Self-Heal and Become Success

John Raniola

Self-Heal And Become Success Corp.

ISBN: 0692801685
ISBN-13: 9780692801680
Library of Congress Control Number: 2017901375
John Raniola, South Farmingdale, NEW YORK

$\mathcal{I}$ feel that most self-help writers have already found the way and written about it, or they are just repeating what others have written before them, confusing new readers regarding the understanding of the law of success, the law of attraction, and the law of life. They may even be confused themselves. Or past writers wrote in code, trying to hide the true answers, as those answers were not accepted in society at the time of the writings.

This is a book about how I broke myself away from a negative, unhappy mind-set and developed a positive and successful one. This book was put together from notes I wrote at some of my breaking points or just when I felt myself understanding what all these self-help people were trying to explain. I wanted to share with readers the attitudes, feelings, and thoughts I had at the time of my transformations and creation of myself. So, you might find that some of my comments at the beginning of the book are different from those at the end because I changed and grew over time. Others have many names for what I call *creating myself* or *creating yourself.* Over the past five years, I listened to, read, or watched as many self-help speeches, books, and videos as I could. I believe many people look for get-rich-quick books, never understanding that what they should actually be looking for are *self-creating* books. If your mind-set is as out of control and negative as mine was, I am here to tell you: if you want to better yourself in life in any which way you desire, you can!

Here are some thoughts and feelings I often had when I was lost in life. Sound familiar?

- Get-rich-quick books enrich only the people who are writing them.
- How can I take advice from rich people about being happy if they are already successful and rich?
- The days of people being successful are over.
- I can't do it. After all, I've been told over and over, "You can't do it."
- After reading and listening to books repeatedly, I have a feeling that I'm getting better, but I still don't understand what I have to do to become rich and successful.
- I want to give up. I'm confused and think I'm wasting my time.
- I wonder why I had to be born into this society and not into a wealthy one.

I could go on and on, but I hope you are getting the picture.

With this book, I believe, I can help people to not feel alone on their journeys to success as they strive to become great and do great things. I have written about my struggles and the lessons I learned and experienced during my transformation. I have written about my mistakes in the hope that others can speed up their progress on the road to success by reading about those mistakes. I am not a writer; I had never even thought about writing. But as thoughts came into my mind, I wrote them down. Sometimes I wrote just a single small quotation; other times, I recorded entire pages. Often, I just penned little notes.

I love to help others, but I will have succeeded even if this work becomes just my own personal become-great-in-life motivational book. I also wrote this book to remind myself not to repeat mistakes I have made or the bad habits and mistakes of others. I want to remind myself that I was a worker once and that I need to make sure to respect my future workers.

Is this the day you decide to end all your excuses? Are you tired of not knowing how to become successful? Are you ready to find a new beginning for your life and dreams? With this book, I will try to help you see things that confused me in other self-help books and to show you my struggles so you will not feel alone on your journey toward a successful life. If I can do it, anyone can. I will tell you one thing: before the day I decided to change my life, I was a professional at being negative. I will also tell you that I will never ever go back to my old life. If you feel as though you should be so much more and cannot break free from a stale life so you can find a path to connect yourself to your dreams, then I believe this book can help you connect the dots and find that path. Welcome to the end of the old you and your search for a new beginning.

In all that I did, I had to fight and got beat up in life. Why couldn't I climb out of this hole called life? I was tired of fighting and just wanted to give up. I always thought I was going to be great. What went wrong? I couldn't break myself out of this life. I sat in bumper-to-bumper traffic; I worked so hard, and I was too tired to enjoy my life. I didn't have any money to spend on enjoying myself anyway. Well, I decided to use credit cards. Oh no. I began putting myself into debt. Many times I stopped living to pay down debts. I took on more overtime just to spend more money. On what? I couldn't tell you what all those thousands of hours were spent on. I was willing to work hard, at all hours, seven days a week, until I couldn't even walk anymore.

I was always told working hard is how you succeed, but my blood pressure was through the roof. I was stressed out and burned out. I had lower back pain, my hip was going out on me, and that wasn't all. They said to save—whoopee!

Was I a living success? Hell no! One vacation a year and I was back in debt. Truly, I couldn't imagine having kids with no money and no time. Yes, I was lucky to have a job. Really? Who wanted to get married anyway? So many people were getting divorced, or they were miserable. War was happening all over the world, and crime was out of control. Was society breaking?

With all that was going on around me, I was also fighting a battle in my own head. I grew up without ever having material things. I wore hand-me-down clothing with patches all over. When I was two and a half, my mother passed away, so my dad got remarried to a wonderful lady. My father was a police officer from the sixties through the eighties. He must have seen some crazy things in those years. Because of his job, he had no fear of kicking in the doors and running into danger. He loved his job. That was who he was: a soldier, an honor guard, and a police officer. I have looked up to him ever since I was a child—even though he did not make a lot of money to shower us with material things. He made up for it with his skills and love for the family. I can remember his love for the country, the flag, and the military. He also loved protecting people, supporting people, and helping others. I remember his skill at fixing cars and things around the house. Even though I watched and helped him fix the family cars, that was the one thing I never wanted to do when I got older. The cars were junk boxes that were constantly breaking down. I did find his carpentry work interesting, though.

For some reason, when I was a kid, I always wanted a construction business. I found it amazing to be able to create something. But my teachers told me I was not smart enough to have my own business. In my early twenties, I received a small settlement from a car accident. Instead of just spending it, I asked my dad to go into partnership with me in a carpentry business. I planned to invest the money into that business. He turned down the offer; I am guessing it was because he was afraid of what he had seen or because of what his past had programmed into him. Later in life, he did tell me he regretted that decision. His belief at that point was that people had already made their money, and the opportunities for others were not out there anymore.

A few years later, I had a friend who was cleaning carpets. I realized that was a business that would allow me to hire low-cost labor and train the workers with little time and money. I asked my friend whether he would go into partnership with me. The deal was that I would buy the equipment, and he would work any jobs that came in during the weekdays. As I was an HVAC (heating, ventilation, and air conditioning) mechanic working in large buildings, I expected to have the opportunity to grab contracts for the carpet-cleaning business, and I planned to work nights and weekends. But after the equipment was bought and the business was started, my friend disappeared and never answered his phone. Because I had already invested in the carpet-cleaning equipment, I decided to get trained and certified for cleaning carpets. I was doing pretty well, and soon I was making more money on the weekends than I was all week doing HVAC. Then my dad asked me whether pushing that machine around was degrading. Shortly after that question from my dad, and in order to stay loyal to my full-time job, I started to turn down carpet-cleaning jobs. So, that dream faded away. What could I say? I was always told the way to succeed was to work for a secure job. Starting when I was a child, I was always told that business was too risky, everyone had made their money already, opportunities did not exist anymore, and I should get a government job.

Next, I tried a few marketing ideas. I sold diet programs. That didn't last long. While trying to sell the diet programs, I would listen to people explaining how awful they felt. I even had people tell me the diets didn't work, only to find out later that they ate fast food all day in addition to the meal replacements. It was sad, and I felt I had failed those people. So that all slipped away too. I also tried a couple of times to open an HVAC company in addition to my full-time job. Again, being loyal to my employer, I worked overtime and burned myself out, letting my customers slip away.

At funerals, my dad often said, "I don't want a wake, and I don't want everyone talking about me, laughing at me, and poking fun at me." Boy, was he wrong, and was I wrong! When my dad died, no one made fun of him at all. Most people cried, and everyone had awesome stories to tell about him. In some ways, this should have been my waking-up point in life, except I was unable to see fully or connect the dots at that time to find what I was looking for in life; I was living in a stale life without any faith in myself to grow into a better life. Only when I started to write did the dots start to connect. At the time of my dad's wake, I believed he was unsuccessful. I had always believed that he was being taken advantage of by family members and others. On the day of his wake, I realized life was not about material things. Rather, I saw life was about helping others, caring for others, and doing what makes you feel great as a person. The idea that the one with the most toys wins is BS. In reality, the one who touches the most hearts wins. Will you have people poking fun of you after you are dead? Will they be talking bad about you? Will they cry, or will they not even care that you're gone? Will it be just another one of those annoying wakes that people feel they have to attend?

Let's pretend you are watching your own wake or funeral. What will people say about you? Did you live a fulfilling life? Did you live as a great person? What regrets did you have? Did you create your dreams? Did you run out of life or time? Write your answers down. Write down anything you are not happy with. Then write down how you can change it. If you are satisfied with some good things, write down how you can become better at those things. If you are not growing, you are dying. Don't let these thoughts bring you down. This is the beginning of the creation of the great life you were born to live. I also recommend you keep a journal and jot down all that comes to your mind as you create the great new you. I also recommend writing them in one book. I have notes all over, and they're all mixed up. Most notes have not even made it into this book. Yes, I was unorganized with my note taking.

Like I said, the funeral should have been my waking-up point in life. I didn't see it at the time, though, because I didn't know what I was looking for. Only when I started reading, listening to self-help books, and writing down my thoughts was I able to begin to understand. I started to realize I was growing in my thoughts, improving my character, and becoming a better person.

With panic attacks and high blood pressure, I felt ready to snap. I had back pain and hip dislocation, as I'd drive three to six hours a day in bumper-to-bumper traffic for my job to work with annoying helpers. I'd nearly fall asleep at the wheel. I was always ready to leave the van in the middle of the Long Island Expressway and walk home. I worked in run-down buildings on run-down equipment. I lost all pride in my work, and everyone around me was always miserable. I never knew when the phone would ring on the way home from work and I'd be told to turn around and go back into the city for a service call. So I had to forget about ever making any plans after work. My body was shutting down at the age of thirty-six and I didn't know how many years I could keep going like that. As I left a jobsite, I would get pumped up to go to the gym or do martial arts. But halfway home, sitting in traffic, it all changed, and I would be off to the liquor store to pick up a bottle to drink when I got home. I was out of shape and miserable. I knew I needed to find a way to get myself out of this world I'd found myself living in.

Find your biggest negative, and find a way to make it a positive.

Slowly, I began looking for ways to break free from this life. I needed to find a method for turning my negativity into positivity. I realized I had the Internet on my phone, and I had access to videos. Somehow, I decided to look up motivational videos. My biggest negative was wasting my life in traffic, so I started to spend that time listening to any motivational videos, speeches, or clips of audiobooks I could find. They started getting boring, though. I had a relatively small selection, considering all the time I spent in traffic.

Don't have a drawer that puts your life or dreams on hold.

While I was working at a zoo in New York, I had to work on an air-conditioning system in a basement with giant roaches all over. This job was tedious, stressful, and disgusting. On top of that, I was stuck with two lazy helpers who just stressed me out even more. To make matters worse, the work was in a basement with no phone service and bad radio reception. (Later on, though, I found that to be a blessing.) Finally, I decided to stop asking the office for a helper. This left me time to myself to gather my thoughts. I decided I had to figure out a way to turn this negative into a positive. Then I remembered something. Years before, I had picked up a CD package that I had tried to listen to and then stopped. I had felt embarrassed that I'd wasted my money on this CD package, so I had tossed it into a drawer. But then I took my MP3 player and recorded all the CDs. Over the next two or three days, I listened to the entire audiobook. Later on in this book, I will list that book and all the other books I have found that changed my thinking and life. I do not list them now because I made many mistakes while reading them, and I feel that if you read about my mistakes and confusion first, it might help you to understand the books faster than I did. This audiobook blew my mind and opened up my thinking about my life to a whole new level. I do not want you to just stop at my book; I want you to read any book you find interesting. My book is just a stepping-stone.

After listening to that book, I was hooked. I started going to the library and checking out self-help, motivational, finance, and business audiobooks. I also checked out anything else I could find. Keep in mind that I spent a lot of my life in traffic, and because my job was mechanical, I was working alone most of the time. So I was able to listen to a lot of books. I would listen to books over and over. Every time I listened, I would notice something I had missed the last time.

The year before that zoo job, when I took those CDs out of my drawer, Hurricane Sandy hit Long Island. The following May, after the storm and before the summer, I was inspired by the books I had been reading to open another

HVAC company. I decided to get a business license so I could work in the county where I lived. It took me about six sick days to get my paperwork in order before the application was accepted. Then it took months to get the license. Now keep in mind that I had tried to get things started in time for the air-conditioning season because all the equipment by the water was under salt water due to the storm; it had to be replaced due to salt water damage. Truly, it would have been the best time to start the business. I finally received my license in November, though, long after the summer was over.

Why couldn't I get a break? I asked myself whether I should give up or go on. I would not give up on my dreams and goals. I would adjust my plans and always push forward—no matter how easy it seemed to give up and fail or how hard it looked to succeed. I would learn from my mistakes until my dream of success became a reality. By persisting, I would figure out the correct path to success, or I would find others with excellent character who were willing to help me along the way. Failure was not an option.

By reading or listening to any self-help books I could find, I realized I was beginning to grow. I was starting to lift myself up a little bit every day. I found that on the days I began to feel negative, I had to go back to the books so I could uplift myself again. I started to like who I was becoming, and I started to realize I did not fit in my surroundings any longer. I watched my fellow workers become really happy when they got overtime. They counted how much they would bring home to pay their bills. The same people had broken marriages, debts, negative mind-sets, and no time for their kids. They were lucky if they went on vacation once every ten years. They were giving up life for work. One day at lunch, I just sat there and listened to them talk. I couldn't understand their thinking, and most of all, I couldn't believe that in the past I had the same thoughts about life.

Money is not worth forgetting about your family.

Some bosses believe that forcing an employee to work overtime is a bonus for that employee. But overtime is not a bonus from your boss.

I knew then it would just be a matter of time before I quit my job. First, though, I wanted to be free of debt. One month went by, then another month, and then another. I had already picked up a new truck for my business and had started to prepare it with tools and shelving. A couple of months earlier, I had taken a prep class on how to pass another county's business-license test so I could work in the county. I failed that test even after taking the prep class. I attempted to call the teacher again about another prep class for further teaching on how to read the codebook and to better understand how the math worked. I hoped I would have a better chance at passing the test the second time around. I made call after call, but he didn't phone me back. I didn't know what to do. There was no way to pass that test without help because I had to be able to read the codebook, which I believed was written by professors. They had written it in a puzzling form, or at least I found it puzzling. (Sounds a little like self-help books.) I was still working full time at my job, and the retest was in two weeks. Trying to study and work at the same time was so frustrating. Should I give up? Then I asked myself a very important and life-changing question: What was my true dream? My answer was to open a business. I finally found the courage to go in and give my two-week notice. I realized that if I wanted my own business I had to jump into it 100 percent. That afternoon, I was told to bring my truck into the office the next morning because my employer was terminating me from my job that day. Others told me the bosses had said, "F——— him. Tell him to bring his truck in." What a blessing this turned out to be! I had less than two weeks until my retest, and I would have needed to take a day off during those two weeks to take the test. I did learn a valuable lesson from that experience, though. The workers were upset with the bosses because I was known to be one of the most loyal workers. I had worked more than eighteen years at the same job, and the bosses just said, "F——— him." Did it change anything for them? No, they are still just trapped in their own negative worlds.

I decided that in order to pass this test I had to have the teacher help me. I didn't have a job anymore, so I now had time to go speak to the teacher in person. He not only taught me but also gave me a free review, and he asked me whether I would hire his students when I grew my business and needed to hire workers. He also gave me some valuable advice. He told me I was clean-cut and well spoken. He recommended I go into the offices of the counties and talk to the inspectors in person. He said they would be willing to help me.

I learned a lesson: a frustrated and negative mind-set almost caused me to lose out on the training I needed to pass the test. Why? Negative people only help you stay negative. Positively motivated people will help you if you show a positive and motivated attitude or mind-set. Great people want others to succeed, and great people feel great helping others. I passed that part of the test.

Another lesson I learned was that whenever you leave the house, you should always dress nicely and display a great character. When you are stressed, no one will be willing to help you. Stop what you are doing. *Stress is a sign you are doing something wrong.* It might be a great time to reset. I reset by hiking, listening to audiobooks, doing martial arts, or going to the gym. Clear your mind, reset, and look over your plans. Create and post your future written plan or goals in a place you will walk past every day. Put it up in your bathroom if you have to. This way, you will be reminded every day to work on your dreams. Create your dreams in your thoughts and mind. Then practice seeing your dreams, living your dreams, and feeling your dreams every day. When you do this, you will find that your thoughts and mind start to create your dreams. Have faith in yourself and your dreams. Have you ever just woken up with the answer you couldn't find the day before? That was your mind working for you as you slept. Also keep in mind that if success came to you with ease, you might not respect it as much.

I had twenty years of work under my belt, and I still had to pay someone to teach me the answers and how to find what I needed in the codebook. You need to be willing to do anything it takes to get ahead. Most people will give up at the first sign of failure or when they realize they have to work hard. Instead, you need to practice, study, and keep on going.

My first job in my new business was a loss due to a bad estimate. Also, the supply house charged me for material as though I was a customer off the street—not a business. I was advised to take the job cheap to get in with the contractor. Did it pay off?

My bills were outrageous; insurance costs were high, and I needed to pay license fee after license fee. I was charging low prices for high-quality work just to move money, and there were business papers all over the place in my office and home. I was failing simple tests and couldn't even think. I wondered what I should do. I felt so lost and so confused. Every time I got three steps ahead, I got knocked down two steps; growth was happening at a slow pace. I made mistake after mistake, but I had changed my negativity to positivity. I had listened to so many self-help books over and over again. I felt I was taking a beating in all that I was doing. What was I missing? What were the books trying to tell me? I knew I could not fail and be forced to go back to my former work. Failure was not an option.

I was finding out that success requires more than just a positive attitude and persistence. At this point, I had no help and couldn't find anyone to teach me. I was even turned down by the same instructor who had helped me pass the test. I started to realize I was being held back due to my surroundings, my world, and my own little society. My surroundings had shaped my personality and the way I was trained to think. During the first test I took, I was so fried that I couldn't even recognize the easy answers. I had probably called the instructor with a burned-out, nasty, frustrated attitude. I realize now that even I wouldn't have helped the old me. The old me would have just brought me down.

What is success? Having loads of money? What is the use of having loads of money if you can't enjoy life?

I am starting to realize that the definition of success is controlling stress, being financially secure, being with family, having time to enjoy life, and being able to help others. By uplifting and helping others, you will find you will start uplifting yourself as you create the new, successful you. It is as simple as just smiling, being polite, opening a door for someone, volunteering in an organization, and always showing good character in all your actions. You will start feeling an energy growing inside you that will start to make you glow. You will start feeling better about yourself, and all those nasty, negative people will start to fade away. Change the world and society with one kind gesture at a time. The world or your society is what you choose to see and create. You are the creator of your own great world. Start creating your own world by creating your dreams. Success is a state of mind.

> *Fade away or never stop growing—the choice is yours. Everyone has the means to become great.*

It is said that you should give more than you receive. Did I read this one wrong? I gave too much in helping people. I am not talking about when I gave to the people who really needed it or about when I was just being kind. Rather, I found out how fast people take advantage of you. Boy, does that piss you off and throw you right back into a negative mind-set! This happened to me as I looked at these people's cars, houses, and pools. I had given them a break just to get the job while I ran my business with my savings. I didn't want to give up the quality of my work so that someone who didn't deserve it saved money while I struggled to build a business and my reputation. Remember, when you cut quality, you cut the character of your business and yourself. You are not just another business or person; you have a great business and are a person with great character. Great people hire those with great character. I am not saying that in the beginning you will be able to choose your customers, but I will tell you that as time goes on, the customers who take advantage of you will fade away, and the great ones will start to show up. Just don't get stuck with the lower-level people. You are visiting that level of society just long enough to receive lessons and answers you will need to move up to the next level of society. *If you are not growing, you are fading away.* I have come to realize that in life there are many levels of success, levels of society, and levels of thought.

It is important to learn to control negative thoughts and thoughts of the past that always seem to bring you down. How do you stay positive when the past keeps popping up in your head? I find it amazing, as it's always a negative thought of the past that seems to be what brings me down. Whenever I find my mind going toward a negative thought, I have learned to say this to myself: The past is the past, and I can't control the past; I can only control the future. I am going to be successful. I am going to be wealthy in character, and I am going to do great things.

At first, I would repeat this until I started to think positive thoughts. Using this method, I went from having thousands of negative thoughts a day to almost none or none altogether. I later cut it down to just saying the word *success*. With practice, I trained myself to eliminate a bad habit and create the good habit of positive thinking. Later on, however, I found a problem with this personal speech to myself. Further on in the book, I will let you know how I corrected this mistake. If you can see the mistake now, that is awesome. If not, you will in time.

Of course, it is impossible to control everything in the world. The two things you can control, however, are your thoughts and your perspective on life.

Practice having a great character every day until being great becomes a habit. Imagine if the habit of thinking successfully and being successful came to you as easily as smoking a cigarette does to someone with that habit. You could do it without even thinking about it.

Our thoughts are usually running wild. How did this way of thinking become a habit? All our lives we watch television, and just at the moment when our minds are at the strongest point of concentration, a commercial comes on. There is music on the radio, and when our minds are concentrating on the music, our concentration breaks because of a commercial or conversation. Why are so many of us overweight? Could it be the fast food on every corner? Could it be the constant exposure to commercial after commercial? You get drilled over and over with one bad idea after another until they all repeat endlessly in your thoughts. Then, poof! You have unhealthy eating habits. I bet you often feel you have to eat when you are not even hungry. That is your habit telling your mind you have to eat. I will not even dwell on the media and all those medication commercials we listen to and see today. I wonder what habits the next generation will develop that will hold them back from successful lives. Turn off the television, the radio, and especially the news. Turn on knowledge. If you find you are watching television in bed and losing hours of time viewing useless shows instead of being productive, get the television out of your room. Turn off all things that make you negative and slow you down from being productive. Yes, I am also talking about people.

To-do lists are a great way to create and practice productive habits. It took me time to work on this, and I still find myself going back to my old bad habits from time to time. As I create a to-do list, I add things I have already completed that day. I also make the list with the smallest steps possible. Let's say I need to clean the house. My list doesn't just say, "Clean the house." It reads: "Clean living room floor, clean bedroom floor, clean bathroom floor, and clean sink." This tactic helped me to organize and motivate myself. Most importantly, it helped me to get into the habit of completing things I started. It's funny how you can trick or motivate your mind into finishing things just by adding more things to cross off.

I also recommend that you create a not-to-do list. List the bad habits that hold you back. At the end of the list, write something positive. I ended mine with "Now go out and have an awesome and successful day in which you create a healthier, awesome start for tomorrow."

You can also create a bad-habit-to-great-habit list. List your bad habits, and then list the good habits that would help you overcome each of those habits. Create any list you think will help you develop good habits to support your success.

During the beginning of my HVAC business, I was in the habit of procrastinating when it came to work, most likely because I was afraid. I went to a training seminar right before my second summer in the business of real estate, and someone from that seminar sat down with me to look over my financing. He told me I was bleeding cash. At the time, that phrase just went in one ear and out the other. Months later, though, I went back to the book I had received at that seminar and found the notes the guy from the seminar had written. In big letters, it read, "Bleeding cash." I had to look up the definition of "bleeding cash" to understand what that meant. He was correct. I was overspending and running my business on credit cards. Again, it was probably because of my habitual fear of growing my HVAC business. Later on, I finally had the courage to look at my income-and-loss charts on my business computer program. I found out that most of my contractor jobs didn't profit me anything, and on some, I had taken a loss. See, I was buying materials on credit and then paying myself and a helper from the bank account to which we deposited the checks I received from the jobs. Let's just say I maxed out my credit cards fast without even realizing it, or I was in denial. Many of the books I was reading said not to worry about money. They said it would come to me when I needed it. I guess I read that one wrong too. I believe that, in most cases, money comes to you when you need it because you are forced to look for it and create it. I believe this is how you overcome procrastination. You can stay comfortable and passive, or you can level up and create ways to bring in or attract money. If you don't worry about money and concentrate instead on growing yourself and your business, money will eventually come to you. Once you build a successful foundation, everything else will start falling into place. If it doesn't, then go back to the basics, because something is missing.

Why does the middle class usually stay middle class? Why do the poor stay poor? Why do the rich always seem to become richer? We all tend to follow the habits of our surrounding societies, families, and schools. We are all taught by the same society that the previous generation was taught by. So we are repeating the same societies and habits over and over again. Is there a reason for this? I don't care. I am going to break free from this negative just-making-enough-money-to-survive-in-society attitude I was born into, and I am going to level up. Stop blaming others for holding you back, and take control of your own life. Stop copying the wrong people, and start copying the people you want to be like. I found that the people I believed were succeeding in life were actually failing. They just had pretty stuff. (Don't let yourself get blinded by pretty stuff.)

One day long ago, I was eating in a restaurant, and I noticed two people at another table on a date. I could see one person was not into the other, but the other one was blind to it. ("Love is blind.") So I would always tell my friends, "Look at your relationships from someone else's table, because you are unable to see what's right in front of you." It just so happens the law of love also works like the law of business and the law of life.

We have been taught to look down on people who have lost control of their lives due to addiction. Before you judge anyone, sit down and take a look at your own life from what I call someone else's table. Ask yourself what simple addiction you might have that has held you back from your dreams. Overspending is an addiction, procrastination is an addiction, and there are many others. The first step in changing your life is changing the things that hold you back. Be great, and practice changing your bad habits into great ones every day. We often spend more time cleaning our material things—which will just turn into rust and junk in the future—than we do managing our own lives and families.

Here are some common bad habits that many people need to break in order to be successful.

The habit of overspending: The more you spend, the harder you have to work. Overspending is also why lottery winners so often become broke. They just overspend when they get more money. Some set themselves up with lifestyles exceeding their incomes. We live in a world with a consumer mind-set. In habits, we become like our society. In copying and repeating the habits of others, we trap ourselves in the same society we were born into. I am not a consumer; I am a creator. Why do the rich get richer and the poor get poorer? The rich buy assets, such as gold futures, and then let their gold futures pay for their freedoms. The poor and the middle class buy liabilities—future rust on credit—which pay for the creditors' freedom. Having either the habit of success or the habit of overspending can define you as a success or as a failure.

The habit of blaming others: People generally want to blame others for their problems and failures. We see this all the time on television and in life. You need to recognize that you are in control of your own life. Create the person you were born to become—now!

The habit of procrastination: This is the biggest habit holding me back. I have to practice and change this negative habit of procrastination into a great habit of finishing and getting things done now.

The habit of overeating: This is why diets don't work. People do not realize that to become healthy, they need to change their eating habits. For most people, this also means changing their lifestyles.

The habit of taking the easy way out: People would rather remain comfortable than take the time to work and grow in life.

The habit of being sick, suffering, or feeling angry and stressed: It is not normal to feel like this. But some people seem to need to feel this way to think they are living. They can sometimes make all their worries come true due to their stressed thoughts. This in turn puts stress on their bodies. Some people will clutter their minds with stress and sickness just so they don't have to think about life. I believe this causes some people to also have panic attacks.

Change your thoughts about life, and you will change how you see and live life. Can it be that simple? Just change your thoughts to change your life? It's not as easy as it sounds. I believe people have been trained to think that life is supposed to be easy, but some work harder living in the comfort zone than others who work hard on building a future of success, which leads to enjoying life. You are a failure only if you let your thoughts tell you that you are a failure. So how can you reverse the negative habit of believing you will become a failure in the pursuit of your dreams?

People see only what they choose to see and what they are trained to see.

All the answers you seek have been in front of you every day of your life. They have just been waiting to be found.

You might believe you are at a dead-end job. Make sure you are not just trying to stay comfortable with a dead-end life and living in fear of change. Again, you are the only thing holding yourself back in fear.

To change your life, you need to change your habits. This takes a lot of practice, and it will not happen overnight. If you are like me, you will go back and forth. It will be a battle, but it is not impossible. Stay with it, and when you find yourself confused, go back to the basics. Read, listen to the audiobooks, and network with people you want to be like. Evaluate your obstacle, and break it down into small steps. Write down the steps, and start working on the list. I find it helpful to sit down and write out all my bad habits. Next to those, I write down the great habits I can replace them with. We are no longer just good; we are great. All that we are going to do from today on will be great.

I am now willing to walk away from all the contractors. I find it amazing how all those cheap estimates I was told they had from other companies disappeared and how much the contractors were willing to pay if I threatened to walk away. Don't be afraid to walk away. You are great—not a hack. Get paid what you are worth. Besides that, bad contractors cry about being broke and losing money on every job. They say you are too expensive, and then you find out they have new cars, pools in their yards, and more. You might even find that some of them are making more money on your work than you are making yourself.

This was when I realized I didn't belong with that kind of contractor and customer. I needed to level up. The funny thing was that a year earlier I had envied them all. Can you guess the habits they have? The habits of overspending and bleeding money. They have loads of money coming in, and yet they can't pay the bills. They are scamming one company or customer at a time. Your habits will create or destroy you. I am building my company honestly, and I am building it to last, because I am great. It might take me longer to figure it out by being honest. But in the end, I will not just look like a success on the outside. I will also *become a success* on the inside.

Look at your credit-card statements. Stop all your monthly payments to gyms and such, especially if you are not using what they are selling. If you don't use it, get rid of it. At first, I was all pumped up on the best advertising, including signs and website advertising. If you are starting a business, be careful how you spend in the beginning. Keep an eye on your eating and drinking habits as well. Every five dollars or twenty dollars adds up at the end of a year or over a lifetime. I was forced to change my spending habits, as I did not have money to spend in several areas of my life. Instead of going out and overeating and overdrinking, I went hiking. I can allow my habits to teach me or to destroy me. Success will not come to you overnight. But as you practice bettering yourself in all you do every day, you will figure it out. I recommend you hire professionals from day one. I thought I was saving money by trying to do everything myself. It cost me thousands, however, and on top of that, trying to figure things out ate up a lot of my time. For example, I spent time on paperwork, accounting, and legal stuff to protect myself when I should have been concentrating on growing my business and life.

One of my martial-arts instructors used to tell us we do not *do* martial arts—we *are* martial arts. I repeated this for years, never really understanding what it meant. How many people just work out in martial arts? How many people read self-help books? How many people go to church on Sunday but never pick up a Bible and read it until they understand what the Bible was teaching them? How many people truly practice martial arts, religion, and self-help? You will come to realize that most people are full of shit—even some teachers. They can't help it. They have been trained in the same society in which all of us were trained. You need to practice and study in the art or the faith of your choosing until it becomes a way of life. It will not be an easy process, and it will take a lifetime to master. We are life, and we must grow all of ourselves continually and not just depend on the cells in our bodies to keep us alive. Our cells also need our help to grow. The more negative energy and food we feed our cells, the harder our cells have to work and fight to protect themselves. If you're not growing, you are decaying.

Another martial-arts instructor would tell us to master the basics while designing our own ways of fighting. Strikes were practiced over and over to achieve perfection. Then everyone from white belts to instructors did free fighting or sparring in every class. We were learning how to read our attackers and how to move around. We were learning about the targets and how to breathe, all while being drilled in the basics, including an anchored stance for devastating strikes, fast movement, the body position to help prevent the opponent from attacking targets, and so on. Did I get my ass kicked? Yes. Did I learn? Yes. Did I improve? Yes. Did I break bones? Yes. Did I learn my basics? Yes. From the basics of life, you need to design and create your own style of success. Feeling confused? Always go back to the basics.

After three years of reading self-help books and watching videos, I wondered why I was still so confused. I decided one day to do some research on self-help writers who preceded the authors of the books I had been reading over and over. I found a particular work that blew my mind. I will reveal this book's title later. It wasn't filled with professional writing that was difficult to understand—or maybe I had achieved a higher level and could now better understand these books. This impressive work also came with a workbook and exercises. I did the first few exercises, and that was when I realized the thoughts in my head were like an out-of-control television set with channels changing every two seconds. I thought to myself: How can I ever concentrate on building success with my mind so out of control? I felt as though this book and its exercises had opened my mind faster than had most books. This book taught me how to practice controlling my thoughts and even to shut down my thoughts, letting my mind rest so I could think more productively and clearly. At this point, I began to find that as people talked, I could pick up certain words and better understand the problems they were having. I could sometimes recognize that those were problems I was having as well, and I could see the answers we were both looking for. This ability comes so easily to me now that I can't believe I spent so many years not understanding what I was reading. I also couldn't wait to teach myself to move to the next level. I wanted the next level badly, and so should you. We cannot see or understand the answers until we are able and ready. Through repeated practice, we can start to awaken and to see and understand that the answers we are searching for are in plain sight. You will see only what you are trained to see or what you want to see. I also realized at this time that I needed to make this my way of life. It needed to become me. I needed to become it, and most importantly of all, I needed to go back to the basics in everything and readjust my plans, the way I thought, and how I continued to better myself in everything I did, no matter how small or how big. As I was typing this, something just came into my mind. As with the to-do list, you need to take something big and cut it down into many little steps. Then practice and organize everything until it becomes a habit with managing time, spending, saving, investing, living, and loving. I am still growing and figuring out all these things, even as I write from my notes. I feel that most writers have already found the way, and so they write about it, or they just repeat what others wrote before them. Most are professional authors and know how to write books. I believe less-skilled readers like myself can become confused by their writings and give up on the books. So I am writing this in a way I believe can help you understand what you're reading faster than I did. Remember, we are going to be great, but it's going to take a lifetime of practice. I find that when I begin to feel negative and I need uplifting, I have to listen to or read the books to help me generate more positive thoughts. You might ask how I can write a book if I am not a writer or a master at self-help. My goal is not to teach. I am not a professional writer, and I do not believe I will become rich from my writings. I spend most of my time working on improving myself and furthering my HVAC business. But I do pray to God and ask my higher power every night to give me the strength to become successful in helping others become successful. Keep in mind that a lot of the thoughts in this book woke me up in the middle of the night, and I had to write them down before I was able to fall back to sleep. My goal is to help a few people feel as though they are not alone on their journeys toward greatness. I was negative and lived in a negative world. With a lot of practice, however, I have become mostly positive. Truly, I know I still have a lot of work to do.

It has taken me three to four years just to figure out what I was reading or listening to. I hope I am able to point out the key words for you to look for or listen for. I hope this saves you years of time and mistakes. I did find, though, that as I grew and listened to the books I would often hear what I needed to hear at the time I needed to hear it or when I was ready to receive that message. It did not come to me in order; there was a lot of bored listening before I could even get hints of what the books were about. Maybe this book can be a self-help book for the poor, blue-collar workers or the not-so-book-smart people who want to do great things. I have to finish everything I start—sorry, it's a new habit—so I have to finish this book. I have also come up with an idea I believe will open the door for others in self-help. The idea is in the process of being patented and will soon be thrown into the universe through an invent company trying to sell my idea. If no one finds my idea to be great, maybe that idea is not for others to invest in and create. Maybe the idea is for me to create it so I can teach myself a new level of success. Time will tell. The time it takes to get the patent registered in my name will also give me time to work on my HVAC company and build up money so I will be able to turn my idea into a business. I believe that more great ideas will come to me in the future. I can feel the energy growing inside me, and I can see that I am finding knowledge and answers faster and faster every day. It is hard to explain. It almost feels as though the energy of success can run on its own power once you get it started. Perhaps it is like martial arts in this way. You train until defending yourself becomes instinctual. So maybe that is the answer I have been searching for: practice being successful until success becomes a machine inside you, and successful instincts fill you.

It is said you should not start something unless you are going to finish it. Starting something and not completing it will create the habit of becoming a failure and a quitter. The difference between people who fail and people who succeed is that successful people have completed their ideas and unsuccessful people just let their ideas dwell in their thoughts and fade away. Do not bring your dreams down into the dirt with you. Your gift will not help the dirt in any way. Let your dreams become life.

Never take advice from someone who you do not want to become, for you might become that person. We are copiers by nature; we copy our parents, teachers, friends, family, television characters, and more. And unfortunately, many of us have been trained all our lives to become people we never wanted to become.

You see what you choose to see. Sometimes you have to look at your life from someone else's table or from an eye in the sky. Your eye in the sky (yourself) is always judging you. This is why a cheater always feels as though he or she is being cheated on. Thieves always think someone is stealing from them. They judge themselves by their own actions—not by anyone but themselves. Treat others as you would treat yourself, because how you treat others is how others will treat you. Your eye in the sky or you at the other table knows everything you have done. It is your conscience you have created, and you have to live with it every day.

Keep in mind that my dad was a police officer from the sixties to the early eighties. Just imagine the technology the police had for surveillance back then compared to today's technology. His advice went something like this: Criminals think they are getting away with lives of crime while they are living criminal lives and enjoying themselves. But those criminals will be watched for years by the police, who are building large files on them and files on everyone they know. When the police bring a criminal in, they have enough evidence to throw the book at that person; the police will also bring in everyone else that they have files on. They will find a rat, or they might plant a rat themselves. So be honest. Dishonesty will always catch up to you.

With respect to cutting corners on the job or in life, I don't care whether you are losing money or whatever. Never cut corners in your character or your work. It's not worth losing your pride. Also, I guarantee you will have to go back and fix it. It will take a lot more time to fix it than it would have taken to just do it right the first time.

People are always looking for the easy way. That is why businesses, diets, and relationships fail so frequently. It's not easy to eliminate bad habits and replace them with great habits. So many so-called martial artists with black belts get knocked out in a street fight. Just knowing how to punch and kick is not enough to always win a fight. You need to know how to fight by training in the art of fighting. It is the same in life. You need to train in the art of success to become truly successful.

Level up. Truly, you can use every excuse in the book not to stand up and start climbing. The choice is yours. Always climb to the next level, and if you reach the top and get bored, create a new level. *Life is all about growing to the next level.* You will start to realize that in order to grow in all you do, you have to leave the level you are on and push yourself to the next level. How do you know when you are ready for the next level? It happens when you start feeling as though you do not fit in your surroundings anymore. You will watch people talk; you will see their attitudes, and you will realize you do not belong with them any longer. This part is hard to explain. I guess when you experience the feeling, you will understand. You might feel you are not there even though there are people all around you. This is when you are ready for the next level. When you arrive at the next level, you will find the people you looked up to in your past level are not growing. They are fading away. At that point, you will realize that life is about growing, learning, and bettering your character every day. Remember, we are going to be great. We are not going to stay comfortable or be blinded by the materialistic lifestyle. I believe this is why they say the road to success is a lonely road. Your negative friends and family members will fade away; if they don't, they will bring you down with their negative energy. Don't be scared. Get out and start networking. Meet new people, and do what you want to do. I am shy, so it is hard for me to go out and meet new people. I recommend joining groups like Toastmasters or other self-help groups. They will help you overcome your fears. Find ways to talk to people outside the meetings. Why? You will find that others might be involved in networking groups that are more suitable for your needs than the one you joined or are looking to join. I will tell you that you'll probably start finding out that almost everyone except a few are full of it. Don't worry about this. You are practicing and learning at that level until it's time to go to the next level. When I was ready, the knowledge I needed to level up would pop up in books and in life. You will also start hearing trigger words that will come to you as others talk. These will help you understand how to get yourself to the next level. The trigger can be any word, such as *character*, *habit*, or whatever word opens your mind to the next level. I can explain this, but I believe it is better for you to experience this for yourself, because the words that triggered my mind might not work for you. Don't worry. As you grow, you will start to understand more and more of this book and of life. So you might need to read this book and other books over and over. When you hear these trigger words, you will start to wonder why you never recognized these words before. This is the reason I repeat some things in this book. I am trying to make key words pop out at you for when you read other books. You will not receive what you need until you are ready, and it will not come in order. This is also why I don't believe that writing in order will help you. If anything, reading out of order is the most likely way for you to learn until you put together your own way of becoming successful. Is there a book out there that can put it in order for you? I have not found one, or else I am unable to see it due to my current level. I have always felt as though the books I read were coded. I hope I can save you some time figuring out that code and easing your journey in your new life.

Remember, you cannot just read self-help books. You also need to practice self-help methods and techniques until they become habits and a part of you. It is as simple as looking at life like we look at everything else we do, such as sports, martial arts, and yoga. You need to practice the basics until you master who you are. As simple as that is, it took me years to figure that out. Business is the same—master the basics to become a master in that business. Why are franchises so successful? They take the basics and break them down into the smallest parts possible. Then they perfect all these small steps, which together form a very effective whole. That is how you have to practice in all aspects of life, including family, spending, attitude, generosity, and skills. It's your to-do list. Create a to-do list for everything. To develop yourself, you will need to practice over and over, and you will have to read over and over. This goes for everything you do, whether it relates to business, health, fitness, or family. Learn the basics and practice until they become habits. How about those days when you drove home from work automatically and then asked yourself how you got home? No, it wasn't by drinking, which is a bad habit. You got home by habit. Imagine getting your mind into the habit of success. It can be as automatic as driving home.

Some people will tell you that the Bible is the best self-help book ever. But if this is true, why are so many people who go to church living unhappy lives?

My belief is that most people don't understand the Bible or don't take the time to practice the Bible. They might have received some CliffsNotes, but most have not even opened the book. I watched a TV show on the Bible, and I felt I could understand it. What I got from that one story was that God will give you what you need after you are willing to give up everything in faith. At that moment, what you need will show up. This is what I mean by leveling up. You need to sacrifice until you find full faith in yourself, and then the next level will show up—the path to your dreams. As I said, I have never sat down and read the Bible. I am going to start, though. I want to know what answers are in the Bible.

You cannot know everything. It is sad but true. You need to unlearn almost everything you have been taught most of your life. Also, you cannot grow if you already think you know everything. I have come so far from my negative-thinking life, and yet I still feel I don't know anything. I am learning as I am writing; I am learning every day. The answers are everywhere. You just need to be ready to look for them. When you are on the correct path, you will know it. You will see signs, and words people say will trigger your thoughts. You will find yourself connecting the dots backward.

You will weed through thousands of contacts. Don't let it get you down. You are supposed to meet only a few or even just one of the great ones. Always remember that you do not belong at your current level. You are just studying what that level has to teach you. Do not forget the people you meet, and always be kind. Just because people are not on the same level as you does not mean that someday in the future your paths will not cross again. Those people might eventually be assets. People will come to you when you are ready and only when you are ready.

You'll find you are seeing signs or answers that make you say to yourself, "How come I didn't see this before? It's now as simple as seeing daylight." This is when you will realize you needed to make all those past mistakes to get stronger so you could reach this level of thinking.

Does a blueprint for self-improvement exist? If it does, I have not yet found it or received the answers I seek. Maybe I will find it. Maybe I will create it, or maybe it is not my duty to find it. Maybe my duty is just to guide others so they can find the way. Maybe it's for a future reader to receive the answers. Maybe it is you who will bring self-help to a new level or find a way to explain it better so that others can understand the steps with less effort. As for me, I sit and write without having any clue whether I will ever sell even one book. Is that doubt and fear, or do I really have a book that will help the blue-collar workers, the poor, the negative, the injured, and the not-so-book-smart people? Will my writings make it easier for others to understand self-improvement, or will people end up just throwing my book in a drawer? I know that outside the book I have helped many people understand what they have been searching for, so I hope this book will be a continuation of that. Writing this book is also helping me understand more and more about myself and the process of self-creation. The only limitations my mind has are those that I let myself or others impose on it.

Success is a state of mind. Most people think success means having gold, a big home, and sparkling cars, when in fact we *are* gold. The more you spend, the harder you have to work. The bigger the house you live in, the more energy you will need to run that house every month. I will never again say, "Who cares? It's only a few hundred dollars." I now say a few hundred dollars could have been a month's mortgage on my vacation property. Manage your money carefully. I learned the hard way. I ran out of money before I figured out how to cut back on my spending. Running out of money forced me to cut back on my spending. That was when I was forced to find ways to succeed by overcoming my fears and going out and looking for work. I was also denied a business loan, which was a blessing. It forced me out of my comfort zone.

The second wind of success is truly like going to the gym. When you first start going to the gym, you drag your feet as you go in day after day. You try running, and everything hurts. Soon, though, you go to the gym without dragging your feet. You get on the treadmill and run. You are a little tired at first, and then you are awake. You have no pain, you breathe with ease, and you feel as though you can run all day. You have now practiced enough at the gym to find your second wind. Going to the gym becomes easier, and it is also a healthy habit. Create yourself in all you do; find life's second wind to achieve success.

Why do diets fail? Why wouldn't they? Fast food is found on every other corner. Every other TV commercial is for fast food, plus there are radio commercials, ads on trains, and billboards. You need to change your way of life, your social life, and whatever else is necessary for you to realize your dreams. Keep in mind that your body is like a machine and food is its fuel. You wouldn't put dirty gas in your priceless sports car, would you? Keep in mind that you are priceless, and you cannot replace yourself. You get only one chance at life. Get into the habit of eating healthy food. Will it be easy? Chances are you are going to have to practice and adjust in order to find out what works best for you.

If you were building your dream home, you would look for the best kitchen with beautiful tiles, and you would design it to be flawless. You would choose the best of everything. Most people spend more time building a perfect home than they do building a perfect life. People spend time cleaning their cars before they even think of taking their kids to the park. Very wealthy parents have nannies raising their children, with the nannies being more parental to those children than the mothers and fathers. Sorry, I don't believe this is success. When did people start giving up on families?

Do you remember having books read to you as a kid? We listened and also looked at the pretty pictures. Have we ever been trained to look at the messages those books gave us as kids? I can't remember back that far. I know the little pig that used bricks to build his home was always the lucky one. I am joking, of course. We all know the third pig was successful because he worked harder than the others to build a strong foundation and a solid home. Just like you are going to do with your dreams, right? Then you can become one of the lucky ones. All I know is that it took me more than three years to understand the messages I was listening to and reading in the self-help books. Only in practice was I able to figure out the messages. But I now see the messages every day in movies, books, art, and almost everything else.

Your mind and your thoughts are your best tools. Your mind wakes you up in the morning. It's what you use to run a business, it's what you use to organize your family, and it is what you use to manage your whole life.

As you build your dreams and goals in life, you will find the plan is going to have to be adjusted at times. As you learn, you will find you won't always receive the information or meet the people you need in order to move to the next level of your life. Only when you are fully ready and prepared will you receive the answers you are searching for. Learn, adjust, and always grow in life.

Get into the habit of always finishing what you start. When you don't finish what you have started, you create the habits of failing and of procrastination.

Many successful people hit rock bottom and have to teach themselves how to adjust to new paths to success; they never fail themselves by giving up, however. If you have a goal, always look forward no matter what. If you are willing to sacrifice some of your wasted time, I believe you can never fail—even if you have to adjust your dreams from time to time. Failure is an excuse for fear or for not trying hard enough or sacrificing enough.

Surely, it is in your best interest to remove all negative words and sayings from your conversations and thoughts. It's not OK to fail. Failure is an excuse for giving up. If things don't work out in one of your plans and you decide to give up altogether, then you are using the word *failure* as an excuse for giving up. No more using failure as an excuse. The word *failure* doesn't exist for you anymore. But you might find yourself adjusting your life's plan. You might find that the goals you had originally set for yourself end up not being your dreams. In that case, you will have to change your goals. Remember, before today, you were living someone else's dream, which was drilled into your thoughts from the time you were a child and into your adulthood. Failure happens the day you decide to stop learning, to stop leveling up in life, or to just give up. I will never tell any child it's OK to fail. I will tell children it's OK to keep learning and adjusting their actions until they become winners or find a team that will make them winners. Because others might call something they did a failure, however, I will ask children, "What lesson did you learn from it, and how can you adjust your actions to become just a little bit better?" To become great takes a lot of practice, so all I care about is that my child is able to teach himself or herself to get to the next level—no matter how small a step that might be. This goes for adults too. The sad part is that children copy their parents' actions, fears, and habits. What kinds of habits are created when children get rewarded for being lazy instead of pushing themselves through practice? Failure is giving up on success.

Unlearn how you have been trained to think.

Why do most businesses fail? People are copying people around them, and everyone has the same mind-set, which is determined by society. Let me tell you now about a big mistake I made when I was starting my business. Keep in mind that I am in the HVAC business. I was told to go in cheap to get jobs. So I did. I beat other companies' estimates just to get jobs. At least, I was told they had estimates at that price. I was told many times, "I have so many more jobs lined up. Do the right thing on this one, and I will give you the others." So I gave great prices and did a lot of favors. What can I say? The books said you have to give before you get. I was unorganized, so I worked for a year, feeling too scared to look at the books. Remember, I am a mechanic. I had to teach myself how to start and run a business. In the beginning I also tried to employ a helper, paying him even on the slow days with no work so that I could train him during the slow season. Then he could help in the summer months when I would be swamped with work, and I would be able to break from job sites and also concentrate on growing my business. I was buying the materials on credit cards and paying my worker, myself, and the bills with the checks from our jobs. I was doing this without paying attention to my credit-card spending, which was a lot more than what was coming in. I also had my old spending habits. Within a year, I was maxed out on credit, and I started to sell some investments. I tried to get loans to fund the business so I wouldn't have to sell my investments and pay personal taxes to run the business from my investments. I caught up on my paperwork and had a friend help me organize my business through a computer program. After it was organized, I realized that almost all the jobs I had done for contractors were losses. I learned many lessons about the habit of overspending, not being organized, getting taken advantage of, fearing growth, not working hard enough, and others. The biggest lesson was when I realized I was associating with the bottom-feeders of the business world. This was when I realized I needed to level up, or I was going to end up working for someone else again. I saw I had to find a way to break out of my comfort zone again and find a new way to teach myself. That way, I could grow to the next level. I also realized I had made some bad estimates out of fear of not having work. Also, I saw that some of these contractors robbed homeowners. They were always scamming on the jobs, cutting corners, changing their business names, and robbing

Peter to pay Paul. I decided to stop worrying about losing jobs. I started giving fair estimates and walking away if they attempted to chew my price down. It was amazing how all those cheaper estimates they claimed to have received faded away. I also asked for larger down payments and watched the crooks fade away. I had financial problems with the business, and I had to sell some personal investments to fund it. This gave me time to fund my past mistakes, fears, and procrastinations, which came from staying in my comfort zone. Selling some of my investments saved me from having to go back to work for someone else's dreams. I realized the crooks would find new companies and repeat their scams over and over. I watched these people have materialistic lifestyles filled with overspending. They were suffering, stressed out, and miserable. They had unhappy families, were assholes to their children, and had wives who cheated on them. I could go on and on.

Your actions in life create you. This is why the cheaters will always think others are cheating on them. This is why thieves believe everyone is robbing them. Therefore, your actions need to be great so you can become great. Concentrate on your dreams. Don't get greedy, don't get angry, and help others in need. Always look at your life from an eye in the sky or from someone else's table. Don't be blind about your life.

When most business owners have money coming in, they start getting into the habit of living beyond their means. They go out to dinner every night, they drink expensive wine, they take expensive vacations, and more. At this time, they believe their businesses are growing without them. But they never set up the businesses to run themselves. Then the money stops flowing in, so they start charging more and cutting more corners to keep up with their lifestyles. They might give up on the ambition of growing their businesses. They start taking more and more from the workers. The workers get upset, lose pride in their work, and stop caring altogether. Now the money is running out, and they can't keep up with their lifestyles, so they take on debt. Many end up going back to work, but now they are living stressful lives, and everything around them starts to fall apart. Moreover, stress is a disease; it will eventually make you sick, and it might even kill you.

To avoid all this, it is important to create sound habits and learn proper money management. Let's say that instead of buying things that will just turn into rust and garbage in the future, you decide to invest in assets so that other people can pay for your freedom and success. Change your thinking. The Joneses next door might be broke, in debt, and stressed out. Have you ever looked at a broken family and thought, "Wow, how did that happen? They had everything!" Figure things out before you are blinded by the pretty lights, and please stop copying the level of society you are in. Success is your life—not the car you drive.

Be sure to never harm the morale of your coworkers or employees. I had a boss who told me once that he couldn't afford to pay my overtime. This was right after he showed me the $50,000 motorcycle he had just bought during a two-week vacation. I watched bosses drive up to jobsites in $100,000 cars and then nickel-and-dime their workers. I have watched bosses take advantage of their workers. The boss leaves, and the workers start to get disgruntled. This brings problems and more stress to the company and the boss. Stress is not success.

If you want to be the best, hire the best. If you want to keep the best workers working for you, pay them better than anyone else will, and always treat them with more respect than anyone else will. Sometimes when you respect someone, you will be paid back—and more. (You must give before you receive.) Just make sure you are giving respect to those who are willing to give it back. You should not surround yourself with people who do not deserve your respect. If you don't know something, hire someone who does know. Always hire people who are smarter than you are. Hire a team of people who want to see you succeed. Hire people who will remove stress from your life, and always fire those who create stress. Do this before they destroy the ambition of others. Personally, my business plan is to have the best find me. So I have plans for training, retirement, and business opportunities.

Many people fear competition, but I work with other great people who are also business owners in the start-up stage. I feel there is enough money for everyone, so I believe in working together. This way, the businesses can cut expenses and help one another succeed. Let the others think the world is in competition with them. The only one I have to compete with is myself.

I have seen many people who looked as though they were successful and had everything but were actually living empty lives. So don't worry. Keep searching, because true success involves your feelings and your thoughts. Only those who choose to stay empty will live empty lives.

The only day it will be too late to change your life is the day you die. Every day you live is a great day to start changing your life. You get only one life, so make it great. Be great, do great things, and always help those who are ready for help. An important lesson to learn is to not waste your energy on those who are not ready for help. No one will receive what he or she is looking for unless he or she is ready to receive it. Trying to help someone who is not ready will drain your energy.

I watched a show about numbers the other night. On the show, they talked about numbers and math equaling life. The show informed me that negative numbers don't exist and are a human construct. If this is true, and life has both positive and negative energy, is negative energy a human construct too? Does the devil exist, or was that concept made by humans? I was never great at math, so I am confused. What is the negative in me? What is the devil in me? Sit and think about this one. You will receive the answers when you are ready to receive them. Maybe that's today, or maybe it's a year from now. Whatever the case, we need to overcome our inner demons or bad habits and change them to great habits. We also need to overcome negative thoughts and replace them with positive thoughts.

I read and listened to books over and over and thought they were coded. They are not coded. They just look that way because you are capable of receiving only the information you are ready to receive. I tried to write this book with the attitudes and thoughts that I had in my mind at various stages. I believe that at each point I was receiving the information I needed in order to grow to the next level during my transformation. I am hoping I can save you a little time by figuring out what I believe the books are trying to make people see and understand. I have discovered that answers are given to you every day in almost all you do. You just need to be willing to grow, to understand, and to receive the answers. I was still working on overcoming my faults when I realized that my thoughts were like a television changing channels every time I was interested in something. If your thoughts are all over the place, it is hard to learn new habits. Control your thoughts, and control your life. "How?" you ask. That's the secret, and you have to figure it out. Don't worry. The knowledge is everywhere and in everything. Look up motivational videos, motivational writers, and self-help history. If you are religious, open up a Bible, or start practicing your faith. Practice in the faith of bettering yourself every day. Practice creating your dreams and desires; practice making yourself happy, and, if possible, find ways to better yourself and others close to you. Become a better person every day; be thankful every day; help others who uplift you, even if it's just by smiling or being polite; always leave the house feeling great; and live with integrity. Don't be afraid to pretend to yourself that you are successful until you start really believing and becoming a *success*. I will mention the works that helped me later on in this book. Please highlight them, and keep in mind that the books I found might not be at your level and might be hard to understand. You might also find something I never found that helps you grow faster.

You shouldn't feel sorry for others just because you are feeling great. Can you believe that some people are afraid to tell others they are doing great because someone else's feelings might get hurt? Isn't that sad? You are great, you are doing great, your family is great, and your business is great. Say it with confidence, even if it's not true yet. If anyone gets upset about your success and happiness, run fast. Get away before that person starts to drain you. Remember, you are a success. Say it now, and say it every time you have a doubt: "I am a success." Repeat it until you start believing you are a success. When you start believing you are successful, you will realize you are already creating success. Annoy your negative thoughts by repeating "I am a success." Do this over and over until those negative thoughts fade away.

A closed mind is a closed book. The book in the drawer was *Think and Grow Rich*, by Napoleon Hill. I recommend all his books. His book *Outwitting the Devil* will help you understand how not to drift back into the negative. It points out the bad habits many people have and how those habits can control people's lives. I also found *Rich Dad Poor Dad* and the rest of Robert Kiyosaki's books to be very interesting. In addition, I recommend *The Secret*, by Rhonda Byrne. I suggest both watching the movie and reading the book. Also check out Earl Nightingale's *Essence of Success* and *Good to Great*, by Jim Collins and Dr. Wayne Dyer. During the time I realized I had to change my life, I was feeling lost and confused, and I couldn't break through to the next level. I read over and over that Napoleon Hill was the father of self-help, so I figured that self-help, the law of attraction, the secret, or whatever you want to call it was created or decoded by Napoleon Hill. My mind was closed, and I believed that the philosophy of self-help was started by Napoleon Hill to reveal the so-called secret everyone was talking about. I finally decided to search for writers before Napoleon Hill, and I found Charles F. Haanel's *The Master Key System*. This book made me realize that my mind was like a television changing channels. This book helped me understand that, with practice, I would be able to shut down most of my out-of-control thoughts, which were holding me back. I also found that some self-help books were written a lot longer ago than I thought. Search on and grow. I want to thank all these writers for changing my life. I also want to thank social media, YouTube, and anyone who inspired me to find my way to a better life. I have listened to, read, watched, and taken in so much information that it is impossible to even remember who else might be responsible for my life transformation. So I want to thank all of them. I want to thank everyone who is helping others become successful. I also want to thank anyone buying this book. I want to thank my family and friends, and most important of all, I want to thank God for his guidance, which I believe forced me to finish this book. After all, I did pray every day for the strength to be successful in helping others.

A closed mind leads to closed doors. Some people believe the Bible is a self-help book. I have found many quotes from the Bible in other self-help books. If this is so, why are there unsuccessful people who go to church every weekend? I believe it is because we are trained in school to remember answers to pass tests but we are not trained to understand those answers. The chances are that most people aren't even paying attention in church or don't even want to be in church on those days. The most important point is that they do not practice the Bible or faith in life. You will feel the energy of God, Jesus, the universe, the secret, the law of attraction, the law of growth, the law of life—whatever you want to call it—all around you as you practice growing in life. God is in you. God is not just in a building, and God is everything. Jesus did say, "On this rock I am going to build my church." I asked God every day to teach me and give me the strength to become successful in helping others succeed. Many thoughts in this book came to me after my prayers, as did an idea I have decided to patent. It's in the works now, and I'll see what the outcome is. Maybe it will just be a lesson or practice. When you ask for it, you will receive the answers you are looking for. Make sure that when you start asking, you are ready to follow through on the answers you will receive. It is often said that if you start something you'd better see it through because if you don't, you create the habit of failing. You might lose faith in yourself or your idea. Therefore, I gave myself a deadline to finish this book, and if the idea I have can be patented, then I will see it through somehow. Maybe my ideas will just end up on my bookshelf, but I need to complete this, see it through, and throw it into the universe.

What if you decided to believe that your body and mind form a temple and that you have filled this temple with only love? Can you imagine how easy it would be to have a life of success? So why is it so much easier to fill our bodies and minds with anger, hate, greed, negative things, and negative thoughts? Sounds a little unsuccessful, doesn't it?

People see only what they want to see. I have found books that others say are the workings of the devil. If anything, these books are more about how to control the devil inside you or your demons—namely, your bad habits, fears, laziness, procrastination, and any temptations you let yourself get involved in that hold you back from your dreams. If you want to see the evil in your life, guess what? You are going to find only the evil. If you want to see love, you will see only love. I do still believe in self-defense training, however, because sometimes your dreams, family, and self are worth fighting for. There might be times when your positive mind-set clashes with someone else's evil mind-set. I have defended myself from many negative thoughts, and I still defend myself from negative thoughts today. But it's not an all-day or everyday thing like it was before I decided to change my life. This is why I believe in the American right to self-defense. We know we can never trust evil people with evil thoughts. When we stop trusting the good people because of what the evil people do, however, it is not good.

I have watched people making themselves sick. These people are the *poor-me* people. It makes them feel good to tell people they are dying, but they are not dying. Mentally, they are dying because they have decided to stop growing in life. I have known people who are always talking about being in debt, and guess what? They are always in debt. This is because of their spending habits and more. Don't tell me you can't do it. Go on the Internet. There are so many stories of success. I found a man with no arms and no legs who had found a way to become successful in life by helping others. People who had been told by doctors that they would never walk again have not only started walking but can now also run. Doctors understand that most people live with an I-give-up mind-set. These doctors realize that most people will not fight because it is easier to give up.

I wonder how many diseases are caused by people's bad habits and how many diseases could be prevented by living a life of good habits?

Why does self-help fail? Books are written by writers: I needed a dictionary to understand most of the books. I listened to audiobooks more than I read books, so I often missed the author's whole point because I would hear words I did not understand and was unable to look up those words as I was driving or working. Also, authors tend to go on and on about the stories of their lives, or they repeat the same writings in all their books. This makes their books boring to read (probably like what I have just written). People need to understand that they are not going to change their lives just by reading a book. If you truly want to better yourself with self-help, you need to read until you understand what you are reading and then find a way to put it into practice for yourself. You need to practice self-help—not just read about it. Learn to control your thoughts; learn to control your life.

Keep in mind that writers look to sell many books because it's the living they chose. I don't make my living from writing. I am writing this book just because I feel that so many people get confused at the beginning of the self-help process and give up. I am hoping just to be a helping hand for you to get the courage to start to change your life. I didn't have any help. I feel that most books leave out the most difficult parts of figuring it out. I want to show you the mistakes I made, not to discourage you but to show you that you are not alone. All my life, I have been great at explaining things to others by teaching on a level that others can understand. So I hope I am helping you. Keep in mind that I am still learning too, and I am still making mistakes. What worked for me might not be the best for others. Consider my mistakes and my advice, and also take others' advice as you create your own story.

Even if riches came to you overnight, chances are you would just spend more money due to habit. Eventually, you would be back to living a stressful, unsuccessful life with more debt.

The first time I had to do a networking elevator speech, I thought I was going to have a heart attack. Networking has its good and bad aspects. Too much networking takes up a lot of your time and can cost money. I have watched people take on too many networking groups at one time, and they ended up stressing themselves out. Keep in mind that changing your life and opening a business also take up a lot of your time. I am all for joining groups and networking. Just don't overdo it. I used networking as a way of going out to meet other people. I also feel that if I am not out there, I won't find the people or the answers I need to reach the next level. I have observed that most people I meet this way are not very experienced in the art of networking. Some of them have new businesses and are still trying to find themselves. Others want only to get out of the house, and still others are just full of crap. Watch from the other table or your eye in the sky. Networking with the right group has helped me overcome my shyness, and yes, I have received some important life-changing answers that I was searching for. If you don't put yourself out there, how can you learn? So be careful about settling for just any group. One very important life-changing lesson I learned was from someone I networked with. He was a business coach and recommended *The E-Myth*, by Michael E. Gerber, for me to read. The business coach and the book recommended not running a business like a mechanic would; you need to run your business like a businessperson runs a franchise. Also, do not advertise to the wrong customers; advertise to your ideal customers.

If you think hiring a professional costs a lot, then wait until you have to hire a professional after you already hired a hack or tried to do everything yourself. I made the mistake of trying to do everything myself. I learned that I need to hire people for jobs that are my weak points and that I need to concentrate on increasing my customers by using the tool of great character. If I worry about all of my business all the time, I will burn myself out. I also found out that by not having someone do my paperwork and instead doing everything myself, I lost a lot of jobs because I did not get my estimates out on time. So hire someone for your weaknesses.

There are laws for self-help, business, life, success, and other things. These are living systems and can be related to everything. Can the laws be written easily for others to follow? Can you find the steps of the laws only as you practice them or as you teach others or yourself? Is teaching yourself the only way you will be able to respect the success you will receive? You earned it. What would you do with success if you received it? Would you leave the world just a little bit better? Would you overconsume and destroy the world as you leave it? Would you build a legacy that would last for generations? Would you just fade away? Would you give back to help build a better society? Would you drift back to old bad habits?

Drifting is when you return to thoughts of your past that always seem to bring you down. It's returning to the habits that hold you back or to anything that makes you start to fade away again. I still find myself drifting to this day. Isn't it amazing how we can remember only the things that bring us down?

If all you are hoping for is to make just enough money to survive for the month, you will make only enough to survive for that month. Why? Because you are telling yourself to work just hard enough to survive. I have learned that if you want abundance, you need to start asking yourself for abundance, because only then will you find a way to work hard enough to create abundance. Using my previously mentioned negative-to-positive speech, I learned to stop saying, "In the future, I am going to be…" The problem with that is that tomorrow is always in the future, and speaking of tomorrow is just creating an excuse to not work hard at my dreams today. So I tell myself that I am successful, I am healthy, and I have a wealthy character. I have found I will work harder at my dreams for today than for the future. Did I put off success due to the habit of procrastination? Saying "I will do it tomorrow or in the future" is putting my dreams off for another day. I am a success today. You need to believe you are already successful.

Life is millions of little habits. You become your habits. I highly recommend you sit down and write down all your bad habits. Next to each bad habit write down a successful habit that can replace it. Then write down the steps you are going to practice. Start changing your life today.

Clutter equals stress. Organize, remove all clutter, and live a less stressful life. This includes clutter in your thoughts, your residence, your car, and your workplace. How many times do you see clutter and it makes you lazy? How many times do you find yourself just moving one pile of clutter to another pile of clutter? What you surround yourself with is the same as what you create in your mind. This is why most people can't think straight.

Stop spending money on wants, especially if you are going to invest in a business. Overspending leads to debt, and debt equals stress. But if you think only about debt and if you worry about debt, you will stay in debt. Remember, you are successful and filled with financial abundance. Be sure to buy only what you need to survive and to make yourself a better person.

Study, train, and practice in the art of life.

Please do not pass on to your children the negative life habits that were passed on to you by your parents. Passing on the previous generation's fears should stop today.

Imagine if I wrote a book about fear—except I called the fear *demons*. Would you find the positive or the negative in the book? Would it be a coded book, or would you find only what you expected to find?

If you are lost again, always go back to the basics. When I am lost again, I find myself stuck at a level and drift back to bad habits. Yes, I'm making great headway; I'm succeeding in some ways but not in other ways, although maybe I'm at a healthier level than I used to be at. Those habits are slowing down my progress. I am way ahead compared to when I first started to change my life. But I am slowing down enough that if I don't start pushing forward, I am going to end up working for someone else again. Again, I am feeling confused, burned out, and unorganized due to old habits and due to not hiring professionals at the start for fear of running out of money. This decision left me doing all the work. Maybe I haven't figured out yet how to organize my life and business. I am running out of money, and now I can't hire the professionals I need. What do I do now? I need to *wake up*! I need to go back to the basics. It's time to fight my biggest enemies: myself, the way I think, and my fears. No more playing games. It's time to battle as though my life depends on it—because it does.

It may help to give yourself a pep talk. Make it a point to stop everything that slows you down. If you find yourself drinking a bottle of wine or not being productive in any way, stop it. Make it a point to say no. It will train you to have willpower. Go back to the gym, and train harder. Eat as though you are a machine, because you are a living machine. Learn to be a fighter. It is time for you to take control of life's great habits and win the fight. This is the day you stop drifting. Maybe this is why many successful people need to hit rock bottom before they become successful. They need reasons to fight. The only one who should be judging you and the only person you need to be in competition with is yourself. Say to yourself: "I will not let me destroy myself."

One tactic I use to stay on track is a letter to myself. I wrote this letter as an example: "I'm going to be very blunt. John, you keep finding yourself drifting back to old habits. It's been years now. When are you going to realize you need to remove yourself from any negative person or people, businesses, friends, family, and bad habits? You need to be thankful for everything you have taught yourself these past few years. Yes, you made mistakes, but they made you stronger. Yes, you have let yourself drift from your dreams from time to time. I don't care how many times you drift back to old bad habits. I will not let you destroy yourself and put your dreams on hold anymore. Yesterday was the last day you allowed yourself to drift. You allowed yourself to drift in fear for the last time. It is time to become the energy of life by feeding yourself with healthy energy that will fuel your thoughts to success. It's time to get back to the gym and become the machine God created you to be. It's time to take off the gloves. The hardest fight you will ever have to fight in your life is in your own head. You can no longer have that drink at night that takes you away from your goals in the morning. You will not cloud your mind and body with garbage food. It's time to grow in everything. It's time for you to beat any bad habits you think you need to survive and stop letting those habits destroy you. You need to feed yourself with everything great until greatness becomes a habit. You are not like the rest. You chose to grow and become a success, so you'd better start acting the part. Choose to grow or drift away."

I wrote this for myself in the hopes that some of you will get an understanding of how strong bad habits are and how they hold you back. You need to fight yourself, you need to teach yourself great habits, and you need to make it a point to overcome any bad habits you might have. I choose today to be done with any alcohol and bad foods and drinks. Do you have to stop all this stuff? Maybe not, but if you find you are spending more time procrastinating by relaxing than growing, think your plan over. If something is slowing down your dreams, throw it out; otherwise, you will find yourself drifting back to the old you.

You sometimes hear about great people in the past disappearing for a time and then returning to create masterpiece after masterpiece. You even hear stories of people going hiking and returning with some new knowledge that changed their lives. They had to leave the clutter of society to receive knowledge or to find themselves. I realized I had to spend time alone just to work on my mind and to teach myself how to remove anything negative from my life. I decided to take time off and just concentrate on building myself and strengthening my mind. I did a lot of positive research and went hiking. I spent much time in nature and alone with my thoughts. During this period, I discovered that almost everything we do in our surrounding society is poisonous. We are poisoning our thoughts and bodies. You cannot grow around people who bring you down. You will find that almost every place you go clutters your thoughts with negativity. Even at the gym, a television is on every wall, and that takes you away from your own thoughts. Imagine your mind is an antenna, and that antenna gets weakened by acid rain, abuse, and other damage. You would lose reception. Think of your body as a car battery. If you don't keep the terminals clean, one day you will find the battery will not recharge and your car won't start. Knowledge is available everywhere these days—even before you teach yourself how to use the knowledge you have within you. Do your research, and you'll find you will understand more and more as your mind opens to new ideas while growing in life.

I have found that the better you treat your body the purer your mind gets. I have also found that it's difficult to be around the wrong people, as they can get you agitated. Even the slightest agitation in your mind will distract you from controlled thoughts. Many people think without ever having had any practice in the art of thinking or the law of thinking.

Poison is in almost everything we do. Is it any wonder we feel like crap? We are poisoning ourselves with bad foods, bad drinks, television, the Internet, and more. Your body will let you know whether you are doing something wrong.

Practice, read, learn, and research in order to find what works for you. Always search for the next level. Success is life; therefore, success means always growing. The law of success is the law of growth.

Start a *future wall*. Put pictures of your dreams on the wall, but don't stop at that. Study those pictures over and over until you can create a living picture of your dreams in your mind. Every time you have doubt, see yourself in your dreams. Create the blueprints of your dreams in your mind. Every day, look at the blueprints of your dreams in your mind and remind yourself that you have already created those dreams. You just have to go out and claim them. Your dreams are waiting for you in the universe and want to be united with you.

I was finding myself confused again, but this time it was about meditation. I asked a friend, who I thought was way beyond my level in meditation, for advice. She suggested meeting for coffee. (Yes, it's poison, but I'm working on it.) After coffee, we went to a store that sold spiritual stones, crystals, and other items that would help with meditation. She thought I would be interested in meeting the owner. As soon as we walked into the store, my friend went on the attack due to a past experience. She felt that the owner should not charge for knowledge. I couldn't really blame her, as I had had that same attitude years ago. Being a business owner myself, however, I knew I needed to get paid for my knowledge or service to survive. The business owner shut down his knowledge. (I could actually see him shift mentally.) Because I have been practicing self-help, I have been able to read people and understand that people cannot help those who are not looking for help or are denying help or knowledge due to closed-minded thinking. I decided to watch this conversation closely because I wanted to hear what the business owner had to say. I was feeling the business owner out. Then I stepped in, and the business owner and I opened each other's minds. The friend I was with calmed down, started to lighten up, and took in knowledge. That day, my friend and I received over an hour of instruction, and it didn't cost us a dime. I put my trust in this business owner—all because he was a healer and a teacher of meditation. (Some might even call him a guru.) In this book, I call him my spiritual adviser. I have found that if people love what they do and you have a passion for what they love, they will help you. Just shut up, open your mind, and listen. People with good character are programmed to help others because helping others uplifts them. This is because they see themselves in others and also because they are still learning. I always listen to my helpers on HVAC jobs. I understand that they might have experienced something I have never experienced. Sometimes my helpers or students are my best teachers.

Meditation is how you train your mind to shut off your unwanted thoughts. Even the slightest agitations will hold you back from full concentration and organization of the mind. Train your mind not to think wasteful thoughts. The art of meditation teaches you how to control your thoughts. When you can shut down all or most wasteful thoughts, you will open your mind to clear thoughts that can change your life.

It is essential to build a great foundation. Why do the pyramids still stand today? Why is it that the tops of the pyramids haven't crumbled after all these years? The foundation must have been built extremely well for the point of the pyramid to remain standing all this time. Why do some old homes last generation after generation for people to admire? The foundations and houses were built with pride, and they were built to last. Nowadays, we have lost all sense of craftsmanship. We quickly build cheap structures and cover them up with pretty lights. In many ways, we are similar to those cheap buildings covered in pretty lights. Many of us have weak foundations and cannot see how truly beautiful we are. How many times have you ever told yourself, "I love you"? Saying "I love you" to yourself every day is the equivalent of placing a stone in your foundation every day.

I have found out that some information and things that society demonizes are really not evil. You are a fool to believe everything and to not ask why. For example, you might have been made fun of as a child. People might have said, "Oh, you are just a dreamer." Some people are always putting others down because others think differently or believe in different things. I am telling you to dream. I have found that it's hard to grow a future if you cannot see your future and believe you can create it. You need to feel it and create it in your mind. I am now working on building up my dream foundation and imagining seeing my goals completed. I can already do this with my HVAC work. I can run the whole job in my head before I even start it. I can picture every part. I guess a lot of work and practice in running jobs has helped me learn to do this. Now how can I do the same thing with creating my dreams?

Deteriorate the body, and you deteriorate the mind. Deteriorate the mind, and you deteriorate the body.

The *secret* is not a secret at all. I could point out how to find it, but chances are you wouldn't understand it or even see it. It's like reading a book and just looking at the words or listening to the story without ever sitting down and taking the time to understand the message the writer is sending you. You might have to read the book over and over, or you might have to experience what the writer experienced when writing it. Most will give up without taking the time to just think. Most will throw something they don't understand in a drawer and call it stupid or crazy. Most will be afraid to think, and they will clutter their heads with fast-moving things to keep themselves from thinking. Most will fear the truth. Most will give up. I hope you are getting the point. Only a few will reach true success, the never-ending goal of becoming a better you.

You will find as you grow in life that you will grow into the answers in the books.

As you seek the true secret of success, you will start realizing the answers are everywhere. You just need to be ready, through a lot of practice, to understand that success has been in front of you all this time. Always examine your life; your mind knows who you are—even if you feel confused. As long as you always look to learn and grow, the mind will teach you, lead you, and guide you. It has taken me over four years now, and it's time to finish this book. I have found that I have been able to motivate people around me, with them seeing the path to the light of life. I am hoping that by writing this book I will save people time in learning the art of life. I am at a new point in my research, and this book was written to help get you started. Maybe I will write a new book about the next levels. All I know now is that it will take time and a lot of practice to develop myself to the next levels. At this point, I am thankful for all the lessons and knowledge I have received. It is time to level up. Be great in character, do great things, help others in need, give back, practice great habits, go back to the basics when you are confused, treat everyone with respect, and leave behind people who don't want your help. Be thankful for everything great that happens and for every lesson learned, no matter how big or small.

Paint your dreams and goals in your thoughts every day, and create your masterpiece one little step at a time. Have full faith in yourself and in everything you do.

It is said that the fastest way to success is helping others succeed. I tried to create a self-help brainstorming group among my friends and family, but all I got were jokes and negative remarks. So I just continued brainstorming by myself. I have found that most people do not want to change and might even believe you are crazy if you are willing to work at success. I found myself dropping friends and even family members. Never let two lives be destroyed by one life. So many people give up their dreams because of someone else's bad habits. I am telling you that you might have to walk away from some or all of your family members; otherwise, you will be allowing them to destroy your life. As time goes on, you will start to succeed and change your life, and you will find you are touching other people's lives. You will be awakening them and helping them break away from idle, stale lives. Just as you need to hire the best people for all parts of your business, you also need to find brainstorming partners who will help strengthen and build your life as well as their lives. You need to create the strongest, smartest, hardest-working master brainstorming group ever. You need to become a leader surrounded by the best people in your field or life. *Hire knowledge and fire stress.* If you don't know something, hire someone who does, and search for the best in the field. It is OK if you are not at this point in your life yet and find yourself alone. This is when you have to brainstorm with yourself. It might feel crazy at the beginning, but just keep doing it. Training your mind might feel useless at first, but don't give up. You are firing up your best worker—namely, your subconscious mind. Your subconscious worker works constantly and does not cost you any money.

How does helping others succeed help you succeed? While you are creating your own success, you can also study others and see the mistakes they are making. You might be making the same mistakes. Remember to watch your life from the other table or your eye in the sky.

One night, I woke up with questions that kept me up until I could figure out the meaning of those questions; my dreams asked the following questions: Why do you beg the universe for things when what you ask for is already yours? Have you not yet realized that asking the universe for something is the same as asking yourself? (As I said earlier, there are different levels of life. Some call the levels of life energy; others call them frequencies. Still others call them thought. Do I fully understand what these questions are trying to teach me? Maybe I understand it at my current level, but all I know is that I had to write it because it woke me up with a strong energy. Maybe you will understand it.)

As a mechanic, I was always able to do my best troubleshooting in my dreams. If I was stuck on something, I would end the day and go home, and the answers would always be in my head when I woke up the next morning. I must have spent so much time working that I trained my subconscious mind to do troubleshooting as I slept. How can I use this technique for self-help and success? What else can I train my subconscious mind to do or to create? Don't be afraid to ask God, the universe, the subconscious mind, the guardians, or whatever you want to call it for the knowledge and the strength to take action in creating your dreams. Become the creator you were meant to be.

This is what my subconscious mind would say to me if it could: *John, do you not realize that when you pray through your subconscious mind, you become the most powerful in your internal energy, attitude, and thought? When you pray or ask for the strength to become successful in helping others to become successful, you receive the most significant knowledge for your book and your life—as well as most of your best ideas. That is one of the most powerful prayers. You should not fear asking for what you want, especially if it involves helping others. This is why you find helping others creates the energy that makes you feel alive, which in turn drives you to do more. The reason you feel lost is that all your life you have been trained to be a worker when you were born to be a creator. It is great you have been awakened and you are receiving this information because now you can see and understand more. Welcome to the next level.*

I am just beginning to feel the power of thought.

Are you full of excuses for why you are not successful? Many are probably living with the same excuses they heard from their parents, grandparents, teachers, and other people they looked up to. Some people have all the excuses in the world for why they cannot be successful. To break away from this pattern, you need to quit the habit of making excuses for yourself. I was able to stop making these excuses by starting to build a good habit of challenging myself. I know I can have a drink at dinner and it won't bring me down. I decided to challenge myself to turn it down, however. By doing this, I started filling myself with self-respect. I also challenged myself to eliminate caffeine. Now I look for things to do, such as going out and finding work, going to the gym, motivating others, and motivating myself. Don't worry about anyone else. Just challenge yourself every day to do something that will lead you to your dreams.

So many people build their lives or businesses by concentrating only on money. Instead, you should be concentrating on building a strong foundation in life and business. If your moral foundation is strong and you concentrate on that foundation, you will build a strong footing for success. With that success, you will attract the money you seek.

While you are working on rehabbing your mind, don't forget to rehab your actions. Dreams only become real when they become actions. I have spent a lot of time rehabbing my thoughts to promote my success. I have spent an enormous amount of time organizing and creating a successful mind-set. But I was confused about my actions. As you work on your mind, be sure to also work on how you are going to take your dreams and put them into action. That way, success will eventually be put into the law of motion. I have found I've spent too much time trying to strengthen my mind while avoiding working on growing my business. It's relatively easy to think, but it's a little bit more difficult to put your thoughts into action. So as you work on building your mind, also concentrate on putting your dreams into action. A great mind is useless if that mind never gets to put its skills into motion.

Self-help can be difficult. At first, certain people in your life will look at you as though you're nuts, and they will do everything to put you down. Who can blame them? They live in a society of negativity, watching people fail and give up on their lives. Even when people become successful, they may be demonized by the same people. In the end, they might not want you to succeed because that will remind them they have failed in life. In addition, some are afraid to be alone. Misery loves company. I believe we live in a society with a fast-forward, I-want-it-now attitude and the belief that success is just having money without a strong moral foundation. You will find most of these people live empty lives and are blinded by pretty things. In the end, they are dying inside. This is why I believe some people take breaks from society and disappear to find themselves. I believe that if you build internal strength and always strive to become what you love, you will reach a level of success that will give you so much more than you could ever have imagined. It's the law of everything. With plants, feeding the roots builds a strong plant. With buildings, the stronger the foundation is, the longer the building will stand. People also need strong internal foundations, which includes the mind and stomach. Your mind is the tree of your thoughts, so feed it well. The roots are your stomach, which I believe is more important than the tree (brain). If you don't feed the roots correctly, you will destroy the mind and the brain. I am not a doctor, and I also haven't done much research on this. By feeding my mind and body, however, I have come to understand things I was previously unaware of. Through trial and error and adjusting my habits, I found that the stronger I made my body, the stronger my thoughts became. The more I fed my brain with thoughts, the harder I could push my body.

You become what you choose to eat, you become what you choose to see, and you become the people you choose to surround yourself with.

What are instincts, and how do you find these instincts when they are needed for survival? If domesticated dogs have instincts to protect themselves and their owners, who trained them to use these instincts? How does a woman protect her child from an attacker who is two hundred pounds heavier than she is? How is it we can do things we were never trained to do? How do people who have never been trained in survival find the instinct to survive when put into dangerous situations? Why is it usually only when people hit rock bottom that they finally find the instinct needed to survive and become successful? Have you ever wondered why so many of us find this knowledge only when we are in danger? If we have this hidden knowledge within us, what other knowledge do we have concealed inside, and how did we get this knowledge? If we have other secret knowledge, how can we find it and use it to better ourselves?

As you read more books and begin to grow, you will start understanding the bad habits that are holding you back from your dreams, and you will have to reverse those habits.

The most expensive habits include laziness, procrastination, fear, not being organized, making foolish mistakes, letting others take advantage of you, and not hiring professionals. Don't let this comment get you down. I now realize I needed these lessons in order to learn how to become successful. I now know why they say you can take away all the money of the people who created wealth for themselves, and yet they will just become rich again, even though they are starting out with little or no money. They do so because they have gone to the best self-taught school. They were forced to figure it out for themselves and understand every level of their experiences. They probably also spent a lot less time adjusting their dreams than did people who spent years and large amounts of tuition money in college. People often work toward the wrong degrees just to go to college, and they don't truly figure out the person they want to become. They leave college with costly degrees in fields that are not truly their dreams, and then they believe they are forced to work for someone else's dream. The longer you live with bad habits or live someone else's dream, the longer you will stay unsuccessful. *The greatest teacher is you.* Everyone else is just a guide or a helping hand to lead you to a life of growth. A guide is just a guide, though, so do not stay in the comfort zone with your guide. There is always another guide, waiting to be your stepping-stone to the next level. Your life's journey has to be self-taught. My book is just a guide, so don't just stop with my book. Keep searching and growing.

Mistakes are your teacher. You pay your teacher for your lessons and knowledge. *Foolish mistakes are expensive, and you don't receive any knowledge.*

Some of my best thoughts have come to me while hiking in Cold Spring Harbor, Long Island. I have found it's OK and actually more productive to hike alone. While hiking, I always try to make sure I notice everything nature has to offer, and I thank nature for its gifts. You have to be careful when you're not alone, because people will bring you down and hold you back, keeping you from getting to your next level. I found that dumb comments or jokes from others actually brought me down. The sad thing is that a while ago I would have thought they were being cute or funny. Boy, have I changed! Start noticing your energy when you say certain words. Pay attention to the feelings they create. You will realize that some words give you a negative feeling, whereas others give you a positive feeling. This was the hardest thing for me. I could tell my friends were holding me down, but the thing that made me feel most uncomfortable in life was meeting new people. It might be time to hit that lonely road they call the road to success. I have found it is better to be alone when I'm hiking because I can concentrate on becoming a better person. I found that when I hiked with others my thoughts could not stay focused; my thoughts would become like a television changing channels. You should not make fun of people or make jokes about others. You might think it is funny, but it is taking you down a level. I warn you that if you are trying to break your bad habits and your friends are not—even if they are becoming better—you must make sure they are not draining you. You have lost enough of your life being negative. I have found that I let others drain me. The hardest part is that I want to help them, but they keep letting bad habits control them. I find myself wanting to be alone because it's time to level up. Don't get me wrong—hiking with positive people is great, but I just have not yet found a group of people who can help me better myself. Even the slightest agitation in your thoughts can prevent you from your dreams. The more you remove agitation from your mind, the more you will start climbing into the thoughts of success. The more time you spend concentrating on growing, the less time you will have to dwell in the past.

Successful people look to lead and help others, whereas unsuccessful people look to destroy your freedom, life, and goals in order to control you.

It is said that you shouldn't tell people your dreams. But I will tell you not to tell the *wrong* people your dreams. The unsuccessful ones will look to bring you back to their level. As for the successful ones, they will help you grow because you remind them of themselves. They respect people who want to grow in life, and believe it or not, you will help them grow in life as well. It's the law. Never be blinded by fake success. Others might look and act successful, but that does not mean they are. To become successful, you need to seek true success, and it will take a lifetime of leveling up. You can stop at any level you wish, but just keep in mind that you might lose your energy. This is why they say that after you become successful, you need to give back. This is the law of momentum energy or the law of staying in motion.

What if you have been trained all your life to be a worker when you were born to be a leader or creator? (I guess you would be confused.)

We all know if we feed the roots of the tree, then the tree can be successful. So why do we live our lives searching for pretty but fake objects and people when true success starts at our roots?

Your life is one of habits, and those habits are keeping you from learning by causing you to repeat the same mistakes over and over. *The day you stop blaming others is the day you start to change your life.*

This book is not for negative people, the know-it-alls, or the ones who love misery. It is for those who are changing their paths in life. My job is not to help you change your life—that is your job. I am just a hand leading you on and showing you that you are not alone. If I can break away from the negative, anyone can. Stay strong, have trust, and believe in yourself. The lessons are coming, and until you figure them out, you will stay at the same level in life. Here's a hint: the secret and lessons of life involve overcoming your bad habits.

The universe will teach you through suffering until you figure out the lessons. Everything happens for a reason. The universe will also let you know when you are on the right path. Don't be afraid to ask the universe for help in finding the person you are supposed to become. When you work on bettering yourself, you will be rewarded, and better things will come to you. The universe is your teacher, and it has been cheering you on from day one.

Have you started to realize that your bad habits are keeping you from your dreams and from being happy? It is time to defend your dreams with the weapon of great habits. Start training yourself with your new weapon. Be great. *Make every day a productive day.*

The first step in self-help is to realize it's time to defend yourself against your inner demons (bad habits). To do this, you will have to use the weapon of positive thought, and you will have to practice developing a great character. Will you drift back to the old you? Yes. Just keep this in mind, though: no matter how many times you drift back, a higher power—God, Jesus, I, mind, universe, self, guardians, or whatever name you want to call it or them—has been your life partner from day one. I am cheering you on as well. It's up to you to find the necessary faith, trust, and love within yourself. Will it be easy? Probably not. Be great, and practice good habits to develop a great character.

- To find love in yourself, repeat, "I am love, so I love myself."
- To find trust in yourself, repeat, "I am trust, and I know the path to take in life."
- To find faith in yourself, repeat, "I am faith, and I know the answers I seek."
- To find success, repeat, "I am success, so everything I touch with my creative hands will become a success."

The day you realize you have the best life partners is the day you will change your life.

If you want change in your life, start by changing yourself. If you are not learning, bettering yourself, and becoming a better you in every way, it's time to shut everything off that holds you back from your dreams. Yes, I am telling you it might be time for some alone time to figure things out. It's definitely time to leave behind everyone who slows you down in life.

Remove the clutter in your life. If you are not growing, you are fading away. Be great, and do great things. By the way, I see a few of my friends are now teaching themselves how to break out of the vicious, negative cycles. I know you might feel confused, but just have faith in yourself, and keep up the great work.

What if life is just a riddle for us to figure out until we understand its true meaning? What if this riddle is causing us to drift away from the true answer, and it's just there to confuse us? What if life is a test? Have we failed? As I believe *failure* is a word without any real power, have we given up on the answer?

On the days when you get your ass kicked, you need to smile and just remember that what kicked your ass is only a lesson. When you understand the lesson and change your actions or thoughts, that is when better things will come your way. If you ignore a specific lesson, that lesson will repeat itself for the rest of your life.

If you want to change the world, start by changing yourself. Find ways to be kinder to your mind, body, and character, and you will find yourself being kinder to the world. Then one day, you will wake up to find the world is being kinder to you.

You will change your life on the day you realize that the problems you are having are no one's fault but your own. You will say to yourself, "No more! It's time to build a new foundation and create a better me."

Don't dwell on anger, on hate, or on the past. Now is all we are guaranteed, and the future is for looking forward to. Make every breath count.

You will never find a true and happy life if your thoughts are full of hate or fear. When you carry hatred, it's not that you hate others. Deep down, you have hatred for yourself. When you carry fear, it's because deep down you carry fear of yourself. So the next time you feel anger or fear, ask yourself why. Most important of all, if you don't have trust, look deep down and ask why. You are in control of your own dreams and life. And yes, you are in control of protecting yourself from negativity and evil.

So many people cannot stand silence due to fear of their own thoughts. They clutter their heads with destructive thoughts instead of facing or removing their fears. The sad thing is that they think stress is normal.

Anyone who is waiting for tomorrow to start changing bad habits is practicing the bad habit of procrastination. To stop procrastinating, tell yourself you are great *today*. Stop saying you are going to become great. When you are ready for change, you will start to leave others behind. That is why they say the road to success is a lonely road. This will be the case until you figure yourself out and find you have attracted new companions. Then you will realize it's time to level up again. So you will travel once more on the lonely road that takes you up to the next level of society or life. Level up, my friends. Every day that you grow in life is New Year's Day. Throw out the clutter in your life.

Stress is your teacher. You can learn from your teacher, or you can argue with your teacher for the rest of your life.

If you can't figure out how to start something large, start it with small steps—as small as possible. This prepares you for training your conscious and subconscious mind to build your dreams. You will also train your mind to awaken and to see and understand your dreams. Keep in mind that you need to make sure you build a strong foundation.

When you reach a new level of thought, you are becoming what you chose to become. I have done quite a lot of research, and what I have found is that the answers I seek are misplaced in my mind. How can I tap into these misplaced answers and arrange them to help create a more organized life? I realized that the more I worked on my dreams, the faster the doors of opportunity opened and the faster I was able to understand. I call this leveling up. Others might call it something else. If you are living well and looking to level up, however, you will be guided in the right direction. Some will call the ones who guide you by many different names, but in the end, the guides will lead you to the same outcome. I believe it and feel it. It doesn't matter what your beliefs are as long as you always push forward and grow by doing great things and helping others. This is not a secret. It is in plain sight, and it is more common than you think. Now keep this in mind: you read what your mind wants to read, and you see what your mind wants to see. Therefore, the answers you seek are in your mind. Closed mind, closed doors. Open mind, open doors. Closed heart, closed doors. Closed faith, closed doors. Closed learning, closed doors. Get the point? Keep your mind open. Also, keep in mind that you might be reading or seeing something you are not ready to understand yet. The person from whom you are taking advice might not understand or might be interpreting something wrong. I might be wrong. I am still learning, and I might be making mistakes while learning.

Everyone talks about Bruce Lee and his martial arts. After reading his quotes, I believe it was his philosophical teachings that made people follow him—not his fighting style. I could be wrong about this as well. Most will agree, however, that he knew something, and most think he was in touch with something amazing. He did not just *do* martial arts or *have* his philosophy; he *became* them. So can the laws of life be abused by someone who doesn't truly understand them? I believe the answer is yes. I also believe they can be abused by people who truly do understand them. I believe they will pay with unwanted stress, however. I also believe that as we grow we will be guided by our thoughts, selves, angels, books, guardians, yogis, gurus, God, Jesus, people messengers, the universe, or whoever or whatever you want to believe in. These are all guides of life; you just might describe them using different names. I believe you should take the path of your own choosing. You are one of the great ones, and the path you choose will lead you to the same outcome as another path would as long as you always grow in accordance with the law of life. If you are looking to do harm to others, this is not the path for you. When you harm others, you harm yourself. I will tell you that you do not have to seek your guides. Guides will show up in many forms: people, dreams, words, or anything that helps you understand how to reach the next level when you are ready. You will be able to see and understand the path you have to take, so you can see the guides. It will be like a lightbulb going on in your head, shining on the knowledge you need to get yourself to the next level. Just work on yourself. Research, read, listen, and create what works for you. Write your own book. It will help you grow, and you might be writing on a different level than other writers are. Some readers might understand and need your specific guidance. The most important thing is you should not skip lessons. I have come to the realization that I needed all the lessons that taught me how to overcome life's obstacles. I just wish I could have understood the books faster so I could have understood my fears, bad habits, and mistakes faster. In turn, I could have learned how to overcome these just a little bit faster. I didn't understand what I was looking for, and I still had to overcome bad habits. The path of mistakes I created led me to the understanding of what I was searching for. When you realize it, you will say, "I always knew it. The answers have been teaching me all my life." With all the negativity pounding my thoughts, I just couldn't see the meaning of life.

I have found that the law of attraction is confusing to a lot of people. I understand that like attracts like. I believe you need to forget about the attraction part, however. The truth is that most people are trying to attract things they think they need to become successful. That is why I believe this law is confusing for many people. Most people are trying to attract what they think they really want or need when in fact they are attracting what society made them believe they want. People need to concentrate on the law part, not the attraction part. The law of love, the law of faith, the law of success—whatever law you want to call it—they are all one law. Use your energy in becoming the law. When you start living and understanding the law, you will most likely find that what you wanted to attract before is not the same as what you want to attract when you become the law. When you become the law, you will find that the law will attract what you truly need—without wasting any of your energy. Become the law, and the attraction part will come to you.

The people I envied in the past are not the same people I envy today. I now realize there are many different levels of success and mind-sets. I have realized I need to concentrate on myself and never dwell on or be blinded by others. I will attract what and who I need to attract when I am ready. The success that I believed I wanted to attract five years ago is not the same success I want to attract today.

If you are in search of the law of God, keep on asking, and you will receive what you seek in time.

Here is a lesson I learned about spirituality. I have heard so much talk about the seeing eye, the third eye, the I, the key to the soul, or the pineal gland. I have done a lot of research on this, and I have worked on activating the third eye. I practiced over and over, but I was stuck on a level. So I asked my friend, my "messenger," about meditation, and that friend led me to my next messenger, my spiritual adviser. I later found out it was not just about the third eye. My spiritual adviser advised me that people who meditate need to be grounded. (Sounds as though being grounded is like having a foundation.) I learned that the third eye was a chakra and that I needed to clear all my chakras. This was when I realized that character and purity of thought were what I needed to advance. During my first visit with my spiritual adviser (or healer or guru), I learned I had to stop working on my third eye and concentrate on the other chakras as well. I had a closed mind. I had never looked at any other chakras. In my mind, they didn't exist. I was told by my spiritual adviser that I had a large blockage in my solar plexus, or third chakra, which probably had something to do with family. I was able to feel the blockage during meditation. I felt it held me back from relaxing my mind. I tried twice to overcome it. It was an agitation that held me back. Then I realized that over and over I had listened to and read the chapter about the solar plexus in *Master Key System*, by Charles Haanel. I had just never thought anything about it because it was unclear what he was talking about. Again, I let life hold me back by not looking up a word I did not understand. It turned out to be a very important word, as you will read later in this book. If anything, I thought the writing in Charles Haanel's book of the solar plexus was a little crazy. (This was my closed mind speaking.) I thought this even though his book was guiding me faster than any other book I had been in contact with. Again, I let my thoughts hold me down. I am not telling you what you should do to become successful. You need to figure that out for yourself. I believe you need to learn how to seek success for yourself. Your journey in life teaches you. A very important step in my own journey was finding my spiritual adviser. I believe that adviser was picked especially for me to help me get to the next level. The dots connect backward too far to be just a coincidence. You too will be led to the answers you seek when you are ready for those answers—just as you were when you felt you had to read my book. I have realized that you need good advisers in business, life, finances, spirituality, and more. You do not need to stick with just one. You are practicing and learning. You will need to weed out the fakes and the ones who hold you down. Never stay in your comfort zone, and always develop your character with pure intentions and thoughts. Otherwise, you will pay for your bad intentions or thoughts. Remember, the purpose of my book is just to point you to a new level that you have to feel comfortable growing into. What I have found works for me might not work for others, and I am also still learning and training myself with lessons.

Self-healing comes to you from within. Your true teacher is yourself. You need to grow and learn by yourself. You will find what I call *messengers* will help guide you. It is up to you (and only you), however, to follow the path to success.

Temptations will be on this path in the form of bad habits. The more you grow, the less and less you will encounter temptations and the more you will find messengers of success. These messengers can come in many forms: television, a thought, a friend, a symbol, dreams, a picture, a cloud formation, a flower, or anything else that reminds you that you are alive, with the gift of energy filling your body. The messengers of success will come to you and will make you comfortable. A spark will go into your head, and that is when you will start to realize the different levels of success. That is when you will realize you are on the correct path. As you grow, you will understand the messengers more rapidly. Remember this: it is said that if you want to see evil, you will find evil. I want to find success, so I find only success. Some call what you will tap into *energy*. Your messengers are stepping-stones to the next level of thought, success, love, or whatever stepping-stone of life is needed at the time for you to reach the next level. Open your mind to your messengers.

Is spiritual chakra healing real or not? That's for you to decide. But even realizing or researching about chakra healing might help you identify some of the roadblocks you have to overcome. Maybe it's just a matter of the mind. Realizing and practicing the repair of your chakras will help you heal your thoughts. Do crystals actually help you, or is it just that holding a crystal or stone reminds you and keeps you aware of the obstacles you need to overcome? That is also for you to decide. I will tell you this: *whatever path you take will lead you to the same outcome as would have any other path, as long as you do not look to harm others, commit sin, or live a life of greed.*

I am now finding a connection with chakra healing in almost everything I read. If you research the steps needed to overcome blockages, you will also find the same steps in many self-help books written for business or life healing. It's all about how to overcome your fears, practice bettering yourself, and concentrate on your thoughts. You will find it works for martial arts and almost everything the world has to offer. Again, it's the law of growth. As long as you are growing in life, you are self-healing, self-improving, self-helping, self-restructuring, and self-loving—no matter what faith you believe in. Self-faith is powerful enough to lead you to success. Personally, I have opened my mind to many different faiths, and that has made me realize we are all one with one another.

Life will send you messengers as long as you keep an open mind. At one point, I was stuck with a blockage in my solar plexus chakra. There was a blockage in life. I had a friend I had helped out a lot. I became a messenger for her, giving her answers she was seeking that helped her advance to new levels. She was also my messenger. I told her about my spiritual adviser and that I had a blockage in my solar plexus chakra. I said it probably had something to do with my mother's passing. The message I received from my friend was in the form of a question. She asked, "Do you blame your mother for leaving you?"

I said, "No, how can I?"

She then told me I was just a child when my mother passed away. She asked, "Are you sure that you, as a child, deep down, are not blaming your mother?" Then she asked me if I blamed God for taking her.

Wow, was that a wake-up call that opened my mind! See, at the time my mother passed away, I was two and a half; how could I know whether I blamed God or my mother? I always knew my mother's passing had hit me hard. I had just never faced it before. My friend, being a Christian, opened the door and made me realize I needed to confront and overcome what was deep down inside me. Open door, open mind. See, I also had closed-minded Christian friends who shut me down. This is why I am a strong believer in having an open mind. Jesus said, "Forgive them, Father. They know not what they do." You need to forgive the ones who have hurt you. The longer you do not forgive, the longer you will be held back. You are a beautiful person full of dreams. It is time you heal yourself. Just start to say to yourself, "I love you." Do this until you start believing it.

I was going to leave the following story out of the book. I have found, however, that it has touched people in an amazing way whenever I have shared it. So I decided to include it. Keep in mind that I added this in the book the day I sent it to the editor.

After visiting my spiritual adviser, I had a dream. I was lost, alone, and walking in the streets. This woman came to me. She was beautiful inside and out, and I could feel her energy. It was an amazing feeling. We walked into a building in which everyone was so peaceful and friendly. It felt as though I had known them all my life—without actually knowing them. It was such a comfortable feeling. The woman and I stood at a counter. She turned and looked at me and radiated this awesome feeling of comfort. She had a phenomenal display of energy that I felt go into my body, and I can still feel it today. She introduced herself as Gina, and I introduced myself as Michael. After we had introduced ourselves, we walked into a stairwell that had missing stairs. The only way up was to take an old, broken ladder. She climbed to the next level, but I looked down and was too afraid to use the ladder. I chose to find a new way up to the next level. However, every door I opened led me to the same stairwell. Even the elevator led me back to the same place.

Then I woke up. Keep in mind that I usually don't have dreams, and my name is John—not Michael. But I could recall this whole dream in detail. Later, my friend explained to me that sometimes Mother Mary will show up as Regina, and when people see St. Michael, they will be meeting someone great. Also keep in mind that I am not very religious. This dream was powerful, though, and it taught me how to heal from a lack of self-trust and self-faith. It helped me overcome my fears so that I could climb to the next level in life. Whether it was real or all in my mind, it helped teach me how to heal myself. So, for that, I am thanking Regina for coming into my dreams and assisting me with the healing related to my mother's death, which I had always avoided facing. I also thank her for healing the blockage in my solar plexus chakra. I wonder how many times in my life I held back from getting close to someone or something for fear of being hurt or failing. I also wonder how many people give up their dreams due to something that happened in their childhood. Forgiving opens doors. Sometimes the simplest answer to what you seek is to face what you have previously chosen not to face.

This is what came to me when I was working on the title for this book. At first, I was going to call it *You Are Success* or *I Am Success*, but others have already used those titles. Then I figured out that this whole book is really about healing myself. We all need to self-heal ourselves. We have an instinct to protect and heal ourselves. This is knowledge that is planted in our brains somehow. It is knowledge our cells carry to survive and grow. Maybe this is the internal knowledge it is said you can tap into. Maybe this is why they say you are your own teacher or guru. The law of everything is self-healing. The law of self-healing—how was I so blind to it all that time? Why didn't I see that knowledge or the next level that opened its doors for me after I completed this book? I feel this is the most important part of the book. Self-heal yourself, and your thoughts will follow. Those thoughts will create a life of success.

I have witnessed adults destroying their lives by living in anger about something that happened long ago. Life, or God, wants to teach us how to grow. Everything is a lesson, and it is all for a reason. Let's just say my mother's passing happened so I could open the eyes of others and make others become better. If I can teach others to overcome their childhood traumas, then my suffering was worth it. I can sit in anger, or I can learn and help others grow in life.

While writing this book, I found it was hard to explain self-help. This is why I believe self-help books are very confusing to some or most people. As simple as success is, people think it is a secret only the rich know. I now realize that many writers tried to explain this living law with a lot of names or labels but just confused the readers.

The Beginning

This time I really am ending this book. I hope you have now found a new beginning in life. I hope you realize that every day, every hour, every minute, and every second is a new beginning for life. I hope I did not advance you too fast, and I pray I did not make you throw this book in a drawer. We are one, and we need to build on great energy—one person at a time. I hope you can see the different levels and the times I drifted in this book. I wanted to show my readers it is OK to drift from time to time. I also know I have jumped around a lot in this book and given you plenty to take in, study, and practice. The knowledge you need in order to grow will come to you. I have just planted seeds in your thoughts. It's up to you to determine what seeds you will allow to grow. Don't worry. As long as you keep practicing being great, you will come to the same outcome. I will also tell you that what is good for me is not necessarily good for others, so don't do anything that makes you feel uncomfortable. Growing into success is not an overnight thing—especially if your surroundings are filled with negative people. I have faith that you will create great things and become a success story. If you're confused, so was I. I still am. Your ladder to success stands in front of you. Just start climbing. Let the ladder to success take you to the next level.

Final Chapter

*T*hese are some notes I feel might help you as well. As I have said, I am writing this in the hope of helping people. Personally, I never liked English class. In my career, I have spent most of my time troubleshooting problems and finding easy ways to teach my helpers. If you're picking up this book and are reading just the first and last parts, I want you to know that success is not about the beginning or the end. Go on. Put the book back on the shelf. You are not ready yet. Just make sure you are not putting off success by putting this book back on the shelf. Make sure you're not wasting more valuable time. Always better yourself in every way you can.

You will find that you'll wake up one day and realize you are in a different world or mind-set. The people around you will have started to change. You will also start realizing that the negative people are no longer around you. That includes friends and coworkers. You will discover that when you smile, other people will smile back at you. Some people will always be miserable. Just let them be. Don't you dare let them drag you down. Every time you get dragged down, you add days (or years) to your journey toward success.

Find a place where you can think. I find it much easier to think alone. You cannot think if clutter fills your mind.

Find the best and smartest people, and surround yourself with them. Always have faith in your dreams; they have never failed you before. Make sure the dreams you are trying to create or live are your dreams and not someone else's.

Wake up early, and get a head start on the world. Set your alarm early every day, and make it a habit to wake up and be productive.

If every day cannot be a productive day, then at least make sure you have more productive days than unproductive days.

True gold is knowledge, so your price of gold is endless. No one can ever put a price on your gold.

The secret to success is that it has to be earned.

When you realize you have the best life partner, your life will become a blessing.

America is the land of freethinkers, free dreamers, and the brave. You do not *do* the American dream; you *become* the American dream. The American dream is full of the people's dreams. It is time to free your dreams and let them create the American dream.

In God we must trust.